Early praise for *Metaprogramming Elixir*

This book is exactly what the young Elixir community needs! Chris McCord does an elegant job of laying out Elixir metaprogramming step by step, with practical and wonderfully instructive examples throughout.

➤ **Bruce Tate**
   President, RapidRed, LLC

Whether you're new to Elixir or a seasoned pro, this compact book will give you the foundation you need to harness the full power of Elixir. A joy to read as it gently walks the reader toward metaprogramming mastery, it's a thoughtful and practical guide to metaprogramming you'll want to visit again and again.

➤ **Matt Sears**
   CEO Littlelines

Chris is *the* person to be writing this book; reading his work in open source is how I learned how to use macros. This book filled in the gaps of my understanding and improved my intuition for how Elixir the language works.

➤ **Jason Stiebs**
   Partner, RokkinCat

Metaprogramming Elixir made me want to run out and write code that writes code for me! Great voice and compelling examples!

➤ **Zander Hill**
   Polyglot

Chris has a habit of seeing past the surface of a technology. In *Metaprogramming Elixir*, Chris demystifies the foundation of Elixir itself, opening the door for every Elixir programmer to build applications in fun, powerful ways.

➤ **Ryan Cromwell**
   Technical director, Sparkbox

A treasure trove of metaprogramming patterns, this book is just what the community needs to communicate the power, extensibility, and practicality of metaprogramming in Elixir. After reading it, you'll know how and why to use metaprogramming both responsibly and irresponsibly. Definitely a must-have for anyone wanting to go beyond the basics of a beautiful language.

➤ **Gabriel Jaldon**
   Web developer, open source enthusiast

Metaprogramming Elixir

Write Less Code,
Get More Done
(and Have Fun!)

Chris McCord

The Pragmatic Bookshelf

Dallas, Texas • Raleigh, North Carolina

EATON

Many of the designations used by manufacturers and sellers to distinguish their products are claimed as trademarks. Where those designations appear in this book, and The Pragmatic Programmers, LLC was aware of a trademark claim, the designations have been printed in initial capital letters or in all capitals. The Pragmatic Starter Kit, The Pragmatic Programmer, Pragmatic Programming, Pragmatic Bookshelf, PragProg and the linking g device are trademarks of The Pragmatic Programmers, LLC.

Every precaution was taken in the preparation of this book. However, the publisher assumes no responsibility for errors or omissions, or for damages that may result from the use of information (including program listings) contained herein.

Our Pragmatic courses, workshops, and other products can help you and your team create better software and have more fun. For more information, as well as the latest Pragmatic titles, please visit us at *https://pragprog.com.*

The team that produced this book includes:

Jacquelyn Carter (editor)
Cathleen Small (copyeditor)
Dave Thomas (typesetter)
Janet Furlow (producer)
Ellie Callahan (support)

For international rights, please contact *rights@pragprog.com.*

Printed in the United States of America.
ISBN-13: 978-1-68050-041-7
Printed on acid-free paper.
Book version: P1.0—February 2015

To my lovely wife, Jaclyn.

Contents

Acknowledgements

This book wouldn't have been possible without the help of a number of people whose hard work and support can't go without mention. These names deserve recognition for making the book what it is today.

José Valim—Creator of Elixir:
> *Metaprogramming Elixir* clearly wouldn't have been possible without all the hard work that José dedicated to crafting this wonderful language. Beyond that, though, he has been a true community leader and a helpful friend. His welcoming and kind nature has shaped Elixir's community and set a precedent for how an OSS project should be run. He has been constant source of help and inspiration along the way.

Matt Sears—Founder, Littlelines:
> As my boss at my full-time job, Matt gave me the flexibility to make this book possible. From a work atmosphere that fosters personal growth, to his support for community outreach, he helped make this book a reality. For that, I'm truly thankful.

Jacquelyn Carter—Editor:
> Working closely with Jackie on this book has been a great pleasure. Jackie's guiding feedback and encouragement led to a work that I'm extremely proud of. This book would not have been the same without her.

The Publishers:
> It has been an honor to work with the Pragmatic Programmers. Dave Thomas and Andy Hunt welcomed me into the Prag family, and their close-knit operation made me feel right at home. Susannah Pfalzer offered wisdom and encouragement while pushing me to do my best. I'm extremely grateful for the entire Prag team and the level of care I received throughout this journey.

The Reviewers:
> The reviewers have my gratitude for dedicating their time and knowledge to help make this book the best it could be. José Valim, Bruce Tate, Jason

Stiebs, Matt Sears, Zander Hill, Ryan Cromwell, and Gabriel Jaldon all took time out of their busy lives to offer guidance and support. Jason Stiebs deserves particular credit for being available at all hours of the day and night to offer feedback throughout the process.

Introduction

In 2012, José Valim announced that he was working on his own programming language. At the time, I thought he was crazy. Little did I know the impact his creation would have on the way I view programming. Since discovering it, I can't bear to put down the keyboard. The amount of care that went into the language's design and the level of power it gives you is truly freeing. It's the only language I've found that makes it a joy to build scalable, fault-tolerant systems. Combined with all the innovations from the Erlang ecosystem, it's a language you can easily fall in love with. Throughout this book, you'll find out why.

We're going to explore metaprogramming in Elixir from the ground up. Along the way, you'll level up your programming skills and discover the full potential of Elixir's macro system. After you're finished, you'll know the ins and outs of Elixir at a fundamental level, and you'll be able to write incredible libraries that let you do more with less code.

Metaprogramming—An Essential Feature

Metaprogramming is a must on my list of language requirements. It puts you in control to extend the language to suit your project's needs and lets you write powerful libraries that would be otherwise impossible. I have a strong web development background, and when I started with Elixir, I immediately realized how well suited it would be for a web framework. Phoenix[1] was born out of the realization that I could have the best of both words in a web framework: a language that makes it a joy to write applications, with a runtime that is fast and scalable. With Elixir, Phoenix doesn't have to choose between productivity and scalability. Metaprogramming gives us both.

This book distills the lessons and insights I gained while creating Phoenix. You'll learn not only all the metaprogramming tricks, but also the common pitfalls that I experienced firsthand and how you can avoid them. Metapro-

---

1. http://www.phoenixframework.org

gramming requires special care, but with the right set of tools, you can produce amazing libraries. We'll exploit this fact throughout the book to build real-world solutions to interesting problems. I can't wait to see what you create.

How to Read This Book

This book takes you from the very basics of metaprogramming all the way to writing your own language features and custom libraries. Along the way, we'll open up Elixir's internals to see how it was built from a small set of fundamental pieces and how extensible it really is.

Who This Book Is For

This book is for any Elixir programmer who has passed the basics and is ready to take his or her skills to the next level. You've used Elixir, you love the language, and you've probably wondered how some libraries you use achieve their neat features. It's time to find out!

Who This Book Isn't For

If you're just getting started with Elixir, welcome aboard! But this book probably isn't for you—just yet. After you get up to speed, perhaps by reading *Programming Elixir*,[2] this book should be your very next step. Go jump in, and we'll carry on when you're ready.

Covered Topics

Metaprogramming is an advanced topic, but we'll break it down and have some fun writing code along the way. This book is broken into natural sections to quickly cover the basics and get you writing code as soon as possible. The chapters are laid out in the following topics:

- Understanding the basics of Elixir's metaprogramming system with macros and the abstract syntax tree
- Extending Elixir with your own first-class features
- Writing a test framework with macros
- Using advanced code generation to create a MIME-type matching and internationalization library
- Generating functions from external datasets and remote APIs
- Properly testing your metaprogramming-based code
- Creating an HTML domain-specific language
- Using metaprogramming responsibly and avoiding pitfalls

---

2.   https://pragprog.com/book/elixir/programming-elixir

With this express guide to Elixir metaprogramming, you'll quickly master the ins and outs and be ready to start writing your own robust libraries.

Running the Code Exercises

Running the code is a requirement to master your new skills. There are just a couple things to keep in mind before you start writing code.

Getting the Most out of the Exercises

This book is designed to be interactive. Almost all code blocks and iex shell examples are built for you to follow along as we experiment together. You'll get the most out of the book by running the exercises on your own computer and tinkering with the programs we write. This will also give you a starting point for the *Further Exploration* section of each chapter.

System Requirements

The exercises in the book are designed to be entered in your own editor and run on your system as we progress through each topic. The only thing you need installed on your system is Elixir 1.0+ and any text editor. Instructions for getting your system set up can be found in the following section.

Online Resources

All coding examples in this book can be found online at the Pragmatic Programmers web page for this book.[3] You'll also find a discussion forum where you can ask questions and receive feedback, as well as an errata submission form where issues with the text can be reported.

You are encouraged to get involved with the budding Elixir community and jump aboard to share your knowledge with interested newcomers. Elixir's website[4] has instructions for getting your system set up as well as helpful links to get involved. The *elixir-lang-talk* mailing list[5] and the *#elixir-lang* freenode IRC channel[6] are fantastic resources for fast access to help.

---

3.   https://pragprog.com/book/cmelixir/metaprogramming-elixir
4.   http://elixir-lang.org
5.   https://groups.google.com/forum/#!forum/elixir-lang-talk
6.   irc://irc.freenode.net/elixir-lang

CHAPTER 1

The Language of Macros

It's time to begin our journey to metaprogramming mastery. Ahead lies new Elixir insights and new programming abilities. Perhaps you want to write more productive libraries, build domain-specific languages, or optimize run-time performance. Maybe you simply want to have fun exploring all that Elixir has to offer. If this sounds like you, let's get started!

By now, you're familiar with Elixir; you've experimented with the language and perhaps contributed to a library or two. We're going to take it to the next level by writing code that writes code with macros. Elixir macros are the game-changer. They enable metaprogramming and make it a breeze to write powerful programs.

Code that writes code might sound like a neat trick, but you'll soon see how it forms the basis of Elixir's own construction. Macros open up unique possibilities that simply aren't possible in most languages. We can extend the language with powerful first-class features, save time, and share functionality in fun and productive ways. Used properly, metaprogramming lets us create clear, concise programs that treat source code as building blocks instead of as rote lines of instructions.

We're going to start by covering everything you need to know about Elixir's metaprogramming system before we dive into our advanced exercises.

Let's play.

The World Is Your Playground

Metaprogramming in Elixir is all about extensibility. Have you ever wished your favorite language would adopt that one neat feature? If you're lucky, it might take years to happen. Often it never happens at all. In Elixir, you can introduce new first-class features at will. Take the familiar while loop that you find in most languages. It's missing from Elixir, but you can imagine writing one like this:

```elixir
while Process.alive?(pid) do
  send pid, {self, :ping}
  receive do
    {^pid, :pong} -> IO.puts "Got pong"
  after 2000 -> break
  end
end
```

In the next chapter, we make this while loop a reality. It doesn't stop there, though. With Elixir, we can define languages with the language, to express all kinds of problems in a natural syntax. This is a valid Elixir program:

```elixir
div do
  h1 class: "title" do
    text "Hello"
  end
  p do
    text "Metaprogramming Elixir"
  end
end
"<div><h1 class=\"title\">Hello</h1><p>Metaprogramming Elixir</p></div>"
```

Elixir makes things like this HTML domain-specific language possible. In fact, we'll create this in just a few chapters. You don't have to understand how these things work just yet—we'll get to that. For now, just remember that macros make all this possible. Code that writes code. Elixir pushes this idea further than you've ever seen.

As with any playground, you need to start small and work your way up to the advanced areas. Metaprogramming can be a difficult concept to grasp, and its use requires a high level of care. Throughout this book, we'll unveil the mystery by going from simple exercises all the way through advanced code-generation tutorials. Before we start writing code, we need to review the two essential concepts of Elixir's metaprogramming system and how they fit together.

The Abstract Syntax Tree

To master metaprogramming, you first have to understand how Elixir code is represented internally by the abstract syntax tree (AST). Most languages you've worked with have an AST, but you're typically not aware of it. When your programs are compiled or interpreted, their source is transformed into a tree structure before being turned into bytecode or machine code. This process is usually masked away, and you never need to think about it.

José Valim, the creator of Elixir, chose to do something very different. He exposed the AST in a form that can be represented by Elixir's own data structures and gave us a natural syntax to interact with it. Having the AST accessible by normal Elixir code lets you do very powerful things because you can operate at the level typically reserved only for compilers and language designers. You interact with Elixir's AST at every step of the metaprogramming process, so let's jump in and find out what it's all about.

Metaprogramming in Elixir revolves around manipulating and inspecting ASTs. You can access the AST representation of any Elixir expression by using the *quote* macro. Code generation relies heavily on quote, and we'll be using it throughout the book to carry out our exercises. Let's use it to return the AST representation of a couple of basic expressions.

Type the following into iex and let's look at the results:

```
iex> quote do: 1 + 2
{:+, [context: Elixir, import: Kernel], [1, 2]}

iex> quote do: div(10, 2)
{:div, [context: Elixir, import: Kernel], [10, 2]}
```

We can see that the AST representation of 1 + 2 and div produced simple data structures in Elixir's own terms. Let that sink in for a moment. You can access the representation of any code you write as an Elixir data structure. Quoting expressions gives you something you've probably never seen from a language before: the ability to peer into the internal representation of your code, within a data structure you already know and understand. This lets you infer meaning, optimize performance, or extend functionality while staying within Elixir's high-level syntax.

With full AST access, we can perform neat tricks during compilation. For example, the Logger module in Elixir's standard library can optimize logging by completely removing the expressions from the AST. Let's say we're writing to a file and would like to print the file path in development but ignore the expression in production. We might write something like the following:

```
def write(path, contents) do
  Logger.debug "Writing contents to file #{path}"
  File.write!(path, contents)
end
```

In production, the Logger.debug expression would be completely removed from the program. This is because we can interact with the AST during compilation to skip this development-related call. Most languages would have to invoke the debug function and waste CPU cycles checking for ignored log levels at runtime, because their source code cannot interact with the underlying AST.

Finding out how Logger.debug is able to perform this feat brings us to the next essential ingredient of the metaprogramming process: macros.

Macros

Macros are code that writes code. Their purpose in life is to interact with the AST using Elixir's high-level syntax. This is how Logger.debug can perform its optimization tricks while appearing like normal Elixir code.

Macros are used for everything from building Elixir's standard library to serving as core infrastructure of a web framework. In either case, the same metaprogramming rules apply. You don't have to make a decision between complex, performant code or slower, elegant APIs. Elixir macros let you write simple code with high performance. They turn you, the programmer, from language consumer to language creator. No longer are you merely a user of the language. You have access to all the tools and power that José used to write the standard library. He opened the language up for your own extension. Once you experience that level of power, it's hard to go back.

You might think you've largely avoided macros until now, but they've been hiding in plain sight all along. Consider this simple block of code:

```
defmodule Notifier do
  def ping(pid) do
    if Process.alive?(pid) do
      Logger.debug "Sending ping!"
      send pid, :ping
    end
  end
end
```

It might look unremarkable, but we're looking right at four macros. Internally, defmodule, def, if, and even Logger.debug are implemented as macros, like most of Elixir's top-level constructs. You can see for yourself by looking up the documentation in iex:

```
iex> h if

        defmacro if(condition, clauses)

Provides an if macro. This macro expects the first argument to be a condition
and the rest are keyword arguments.
...
```

You might be wondering what the advantage is of Elixir using macros for its own constructs, since you get by fine in most languages without this structure. The most powerful advantage is that macros allow you to extend the language with your own keywords while using existing macros as building blocks.

The best way to think about metaprogramming in Elixir is to throw away the notion of rigid keywords and opaque language internals. Elixir was designed with extension in mind. The language is open to your exploration and custom features. This is what makes metaprogramming in Elixir so pleasantly natural.

Tying It All Together

We've seen how Elixir itself is built with macros and how to use quote to return the AST representation of any expression. Now let's fit the pieces together. The most important takeaway is that macros receive ASTs as arguments and provide ASTs as return values. By writing macros, you are building ASTs using Elixir's high-level syntax.

To see this in action, let's write a macro that can print the spoken form of an Elixir mathematical expression, such as 5 + 2, when calculating a result. In most languages, we would have to parse a string expression into something digestible by our program. With Elixir, we can access the representation of expressions directly with macros.

Our first step is to examine the AST structure of some example expressions that our macro will accept. Let's head back over to iex and quote a few expressions. Go ahead and try out a few of your own to get a better sense of the AST's structure.

```
iex> quote do: 5 + 2
{:+, [context: Elixir, import: Kernel], [5, 2]}

iex)> quote do: 1 * 2 + 3
{:+, [context: Elixir, import: Kernel],
 [{:*, [context: Elixir, import: Kernel], [1, 2]}, 3]}
```

The AST for 5 + 2 and 1 * 2 + 3 produced a straightforward tuple structure. We received the atoms :+ and :* representing operators, and the left-hand side and right-hand side values in the last element. These tuple structures are the direct representation of their high-level Elixir counterparts.

Now that we know how our expressions are represented, let's define our first macro to see how the AST ties in. We'll define a Math module with a say macro that can print any mathematical expression in natural language when calculating the result.

Create a math.exs file in your favorite editor and add the following code to it:

```
macros/math.exs
Line 1  defmodule Math do

          # {:+, [context: Elixir, import: Kernel], [5, 2]}
          defmacro say({:+, _, [lhs, rhs]}) do
    5       quote do
              lhs = unquote(lhs)
              rhs = unquote(rhs)
              result = lhs + rhs
              IO.puts "#{lhs} plus #{rhs} is #{result}"
   10         result
            end
          end

          # {:*, [context: Elixir, import: Kernel], [8, 3]}
   15     defmacro say({:*, _, [lhs, rhs]}) do
            quote do
              lhs = unquote(lhs)
              rhs = unquote(rhs)
              result = lhs * rhs
   20         IO.puts "#{lhs} times #{rhs} is #{result}"
              result
            end
          end
        end
```

Now let's load the module up in iex and try it out:

```
iex> c "math.exs"
[Math]

iex> require Math
nil

iex> Math.say 5 + 2
5 plus 2 is 7
7

iex> Math.say 18 * 4
18 times 4 is 72
72
```

Let's break down the code. Since we know macros receive the AST representation of the arguments we pass to them, we pattern matched directly on the AST to determine which say definition to invoke. On lines 4 and 15, we can see that macros, like functions, can have multiple signatures. Having the example representation from our quoted results allowed us to easily bind the left- and right-hand side values to variables and print a message accordingly.

To complete the macro, we used quote to return an AST for the caller to replace our Math.say invocations. Here we also used unquote for the first time. We'll expand on quote and unquote in detail in a moment. For now, all you need to know is these two macros work together to help you build ASTs while keeping track of where your code executes.

With the essential concepts out of the way, we can now move into the deeper details of Elixir's metaprogramming system. You've seen that macros and ASTs work together, now let's find out how. But first, there's something we need to discuss.

Macro Rules

Before we write more complex macros, we need to review a couple of rules to temper our expectations. Macros give us awesome power, but with great power comes great responsibility.

Rule 1: Don't Write Macros

You may hear this rule touted loudly when talking with others about metaprogramming. Often it's unfounded, but before we get too carried away, we have to remember that writing code to produce code requires special care. It's easy to get caught in our own web of code generation, and many have been bitten by reckless complexity. When taken too far, macros can make programs difficult to debug and reason about. There should always be a clear advantage when we attack problems with metaprogramming. In many cases, standard function definitions are a superior choice if code generation is not required.

Rule 2: Use Macros Gratuitously

Metaprogramming is sometimes framed as complex and fragile. Together, we'll dispel these myths by producing robust, clear programs that offer productive advantages in a fraction of the required code. It's important to avoid letting the potential for abuse scare you away from fully exploring Elixir's macro system. The best way to learn metaprogramming is to throw away your preconceived notions and explore with a curious and open mind. You can't be afraid to be a little irresponsible while you're learning.

It's important to keep this duality in mind when writing macros. Along our metaprogramming journey, you'll see how to apply your sharp skills responsibly and look at common pitfalls to avoid. Great code speaks for itself, and we'll be writing plenty of it.

The Abstract Syntax Tree—Demystified

It's time to explore the AST in depth to learn the different ways your source code is represented. You might be tempted to jump in and start writing macros at this point, but truly understanding the AST is essential as you get into advanced metaprogramming. Once we uncover the nuances, you'll find your Elixir code is much closer to the AST than you might have imagined. This revelation will change the way you think about solving problems and drive your macro design decisions going forward. After reviewing the finer details of the AST, you'll be ready to begin the metaprogramming exercises. So hang in there. You'll be creating new language features before you know it.

The Structure of the AST

Every expression you write in Elixir breaks down to a three-element tuple in the AST. You often rely on this uniform breakdown when pattern matching arguments in macros. We already used this technique in our Math.say definitions in *Tying It All Together*, on page 5.

```
defmacro say({:+, _, [lhs, rhs]}) do
```

Since we know that an expression like 5 + 2 turns into the tuple {:+, [...], [5, 2]}, we pattern matched directly against the AST to determine the meaning of each calculation. Let's quote a couple more complex expressions to see how entire Elixir programs are structured in the AST.

Type the following into iex:

```
iex> quote do: (5 * 2) - 1 + 7
{:+, [context: Elixir, import: Kernel],
 [{:-, [context: Elixir, import: Kernel],
   [{:*, [context: Elixir, import: Kernel], [5, 2]}, 1]}, 7]}

iex> quote do
...>    defmodule MyModule do
...>      def hello, do: "World"
...>    end
...> end
{:defmodule, [context: Elixir, import: Kernel],
 [{:__aliases__, [alias: false], [:MyModule]},
  [do: {:def, [context: Elixir, import: Kernel],
   [{:hello, [context: Elixir], Elixir}, [do: "World"]]}]]}
```

You can see that a stacking tuple was produced from each quoted expression. Our first example shows the familiar structures used by our Math.say macro, but multiple tuples are stacked into an embedded tree to represent the entire expression. The result of the second example shows how an entire Elixir module is represented by a simple AST.

All along, the code you've written in Elixir has been represented by this simple uniform structure. Understanding this structure requires just a few simple rules. All Elixir code is represented as a series of three-element tuples with the following format:

- The first element is an atom denoting the function call, or another tuple, representing a nested node in the AST.
- The second element represents metadata about the expression.
- The third element is a list of arguments for the function call.

Let's apply this insight to break down the AST of (5 * 2) - 1 + 7 in our previous example:

```
iex(1)> quote do: (5 * 2) - 1 + 7
{:+, [context: Elixir, import: Kernel],
 [{:-, [context: Elixir, import: Kernel],
   [{:*, [context: Elixir, import: Kernel], [5, 2]}, 1]}, 7]}
```

We can see that the AST forms a tree of functions and arguments. Let's format this output to better see the tree structure it represents.

quote do: (5 * 2) - 1 + 7

```
        +
        |
        |---- -
        |     |---- *
        |     |     |---- 5
        |     |     |---- 2
        |     |---- 1
        |---- 7
```

```
{:+, [...],
 [{:-, [...],
   [{:*, [...], [5,
                 2]},
    1]},
  7]}
```

Let's start from the end of the AST and work our way up. The root AST node is the + operator, and its arguments are the number 7 combined with another nested node in the tree. We can see that the nested nodes contain our (5 * 2) expression, whose results are applied to the - 1 branch. You also might recall that 5 * 2 in Elixir is just syntactic sugar for Kernel.*(5, 2). This makes our quoted results even easier to decode. The atom :* is the function call to perform, and the metadata tells us that it has been imported from Kernel. The last element [5, 2] is the list of arguments for the Kernel.*/2 function. Entire programs are represented in this way as a simple tree of Elixir tuples.

High-Level Syntax vs. Low-level AST

To understand the design decisions behind Elixir's syntax and the AST, it's helpful to compare it to other languages where the AST takes center stage. In some languages, such as flavors of Lisp (see http://common-lisp.net), source is written directly as an AST, using parentheses to form expressions. If you look closely, you can see how Elixir operates at a layer just above this format.

Lisp:	Elixir (metadata truncated):
(+ (* 2 3) 1)	**quote do**: 2 * 3 + 1
	{:+, _, [{:*, _, [2, 3]}, 1]}

If you compare the Elixir AST with Lisp source code, you can see that the structure is nearly identical if we replaced brackets with parentheses. The beauty of Elixir is that the transformation from high-level source to low-level AST requires only a simple quote invocation. With Lisp, you have all the power of a programmable AST at the cost of a less natural and flexible syntax. José's revolutionary insight was to separate the syntax from the AST. In Elixir, you get the best of both worlds: a programmable AST with a high-level syntax to perform all the work.

AST Literals

When you begin exploring how Elixir source is represented by the AST, sometimes the results of quoted expressions can be confusing and can appear irregular. You can avoid confusion by realizing that several literals in Elixir have the same representation within the AST and high-level source. This includes atoms, integers, floats, lists, strings, and any two-element tuples containing the former types. For example, all of the following literals return themselves when quoted:

```
iex> quote do: :atom
:atom
iex> quote do: 123
123
iex> quote do: 3.14
3.14
iex> quote do: [1, 2, 3]
[1, 2, 3]
iex> quote do: "string"
"string"
iex> quote do: {:ok, 1}
{:ok, 1}
iex> quote do: {:ok, [1, 2, 3]}
{:ok, [1, 2, 3]}
```

If we pass any of the previous examples to a macro, the macro receives the literal arguments instead of an abstract representation. If we quote other types, you can see that an abstract form is returned.

```
iex> quote do: %{a: 1, b: 2}
{:%{}, [], [a: 1, b: 2]}
iex> quote do: Enum
{:__aliases__, [alias: false], [:Enum]}
```

Our quoted results show the two different ways Elixir types are represented in the AST. Some values are passed through as is, while more complex types are returned as a quoted expression. It's helpful to keep AST literals in mind when writing macros to avoid confusion about whether our arguments are received in abstract form.

Now that we've laid a foundation by uncovering the structure of the AST, it's time to move on to code-generation exercises and apply our new insight. Next, we'll explore how to transform the AST using Elixir's macro system.

Macros: The Building Blocks of Elixir

It's time to get our hands dirty and see what macros are all about. You've been promised custom language features, so let's start small by re-creating an essential Elixir feature. From there, we'll expose a few fundamental macro features and see how the AST ties in.

Re-Creating Elixir's unless Macro

Let's pretend for a moment that Elixir lacks a built-in unless construct. In most languages, we would have to settle for if! expressions and learn to accept this syntactic shortcoming.

Fortunately for us, Elixir isn't like most languages. Let's define our own unless macro, using if as a building block of our implementation. Macros must be defined within modules, so let's define a ControlFlow module. Head back to your editor and create the following unless.exs file:

```
macros/unless.exs
Line 1  defmodule ControlFlow do
     2    defmacro unless(expression, do: block) do
     3      quote do
     4        if !unquote(expression), do: unquote(block)
     5      end
     6    end
     7  end
```

Now open up iex in the same directory and let's try it out:

```
iex> c "unless.exs"
[ControlFlow]

iex> require ControlFlow
nil

iex> ControlFlow.unless 2 == 5, do: "block entered"
"block entered"

iex> ControlFlow.unless 5 == 5 do
...>    "block entered"
...> end
nil
```

We must first require ControlFlow before invoking its macros in cases where the module hasn't already been imported. Since macros receive the AST representation of arguments, we can accept any valid Elixir expression as the first argument to unless on line 2. In our second argument, we can pattern match directly on the provided do/end block and bind its AST value to a variable. Remember, a macro's purpose in life is to take in an AST representation and return an AST representation, so we immediately begin a quote to return an AST. Within the quote, we perform a single line of code generation, transforming the unless keyword into an if ! expression:

```
quote do
  if !unquote(expression), do: unquote(block)
end
```

This transformation is referred to as macro *expansion*. The final AST returned from unless is expanded within the caller's context at compile time. The produced code will contain if ! expressions anywhere unless was used. Here we also used the unquote macro that we first saw in our Math.say definition.

unquote

The unquote macro allows values to be injected into an AST that is being defined. You can think of quote/unquote as string interpolation for code. If you were building up a string and needed to inject the value of a variable into that string, you would interpolate it. The same goes when constructing an AST. We use quote to begin generating an AST and unquote to inject values from an outside context. This allows the outside bound variables, expression and block, to be injected directly into our if ! transformation.

Let's try this out. We'll use Code.eval_quoted to directly evaluate an AST and return the result. Enter the following series of expressions into iex and examine the differences as we evaluate each variable:

```
Line 1   iex> number = 5
      -  5
      -
      -  iex> ast = quote do
      5  ...>   number * 10
      -  ...> end
      -  {:*, [context: Elixir, import: Kernel], [{:number, [], Elixir}, 10]}
      -
      -  iex> Code.eval_quoted ast
      10 ** (CompileError) nofile:1: undefined function number/0
      -
      -  iex> ast = quote do
      -  ...>   unquote(number) * 10
      -  ...> end
      15 {:*, [context: Elixir, import: Kernel], [5, 10]}
      -
      -  iex> Code.eval_quoted ast
      -  {50, []}
```

In our first quoted result on line 7, notice how the value of number was not injected into the returned AST. Instead, the AST for a local number reference was provided, which threw an undefined error when evaluated. To fix this, we properly injected number into the quoted context by using unquote on line 13. Evaluating the final AST returns the correct result.

With unquote, we have another essential metaprogramming tool under our belt. The quote and unquote macros pair together to let you build ASTs without fumbling with the AST by hand.

Macro Expansion

Let's dive deeper into Elixir's internals by finding out what exactly happens to macros at compile time. When the compiler encounters a macro, it recursively expands it until the code no longer contains any macro calls. Use Figure 1, *How Elixir Expands Macros*, on page 14 to take a high-level walk through this process for a simple ControlFlow.unless expression.

The diagram shows the compiler's decision process as it encounters macros in the AST. If it finds a macro, it expands it. If the expanded code also contains macros, those get expanded as well. This expansion recursively executes until all macros have been fully expanded into their final generated code. Now imagine the following block of code being encountered by the compiler:

```
ControlFlow.unless 2 == 5 do
  "block entered"
end
```

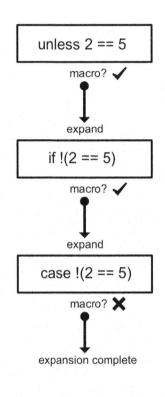

Figure 1—How Elixir Expands Macros

We know that our ControlFlow.unless macro generates an if ! expression, so the compiler would expand the block into the following code:

```
if !(2 == 5) do
  "block entered"
end
```

Now the compiler sees an if macro and continues expanding the code. You may not know it yet, but Elixir's if macro is implemented internally as a case expression. So the final expansion becomes the basic case block.

```
case !(2 == 5) do
  x when x in [false, nil] ->
    nil
  _ ->
    "block entered"
end
```

Now that the code no longer contains expandable macros, the compiler is finished and would continue compiling the rest of our program. The case macro is a member of a small set of special macros, located in the aptly named Kernel.SpecialForms. These macros are fundamental building blocks in Elixir that cannot be overridden. They also represent the end of the road for macro expansion.

Let's head back over to iex and see how the AST is expanded during our previous walkthrough. We'll use Macro.expand_once to expand an AST a single time while capturing the result of each step. Be sure to launch iex in the same directory that you created your unless.exs file and enter the following series of expressions:

```
Line 1  iex> c "macros/unless.exs"
   -    [ControlFlow]

   -    iex> require ControlFlow
   5    nil

   -    iex> ast = quote do
   -    ...>    ControlFlow.unless 2 == 5, do: "block entered"
   -    ...> end
  10    {{:., [], [{:__aliases__, [alias: false], [:ControlFlow]}, :unless]}, [],
   -     [{:==, [context: Elixir, import: Kernel], [2, 5]}, [do: "block entered"]]}

   -    iex> expanded_once = Macro.expand_once(ast, __ENV__)
   -    {:if, [context: ControlFlow, import: Kernel],
  15     [{:!, [context: ControlFlow, import: Kernel],
   -       [{:==, [context: Elixir, import: Kernel], [2, 5]}]}, [do: "block entered"]]}

   -    iex> expanded_fully = Macro.expand_once(expanded_once, __ENV__)
   -    {:case, [optimize_boolean: true],
  20     [{:!, [context: ControlFlow, import: Kernel],
   -       [{:==, [context: Elixir, import: Kernel], [2, 5]}]},
   -      [do: [{:->, [],
   -        [[{:when, [],
   -          [{:x, [counter: 4], Kernel},
  25            {:in, [context: Kernel, import: Kernel],
   -              [{:x, [counter: 4], Kernel}, [false, nil]]}]}], nil]},
   -        {:->, [], [[{:_, [], Kernel}], "block entered"]}]]]}
```

On line 7, we quoted a simple invocation of our unless macro. Next, we used Macro.expand_once on line 13 to expand the macro a single time. We can see that expanded_once AST was transformed into an if! expression, as we implemented in our unless definition. Finally, we fully expanded the macro on line 18. The expanded_fully AST verifies that if in Elixir boils down to a case expression as the fundamental control flow structure.

These exercises showed off the building-block nature of Elixir's macro system. We went three levels deep into code construction and relied on simple AST transformations to produce the final result. Elixir code is macros all the way down. This is what allows the language itself to be mostly built from the same macros you can write in your own libraries.

If multiple levels of code expansion sound unsafe, you don't need to worry. Elixir keeps us safe during macro execution. Let's see how.

Code Injection and the Caller's Context

Macros don't just generate code for the caller, they inject it. We call the place where code is injected a *context*. A context is the scope of the caller's bindings, imports, and aliases. To the caller of a macro, the context is precious. It holds your view of the world, and by virtue of immutability, you don't expect your variables, imports, and aliases to change out from underneath you.

Elixir macros strike an excellent balance for safeguarding your context while allowing explicit access where neccesary. Let's see how to inject code safely and the available tools to reach into the caller's context when necessary.

Injecting Code

Because macros are all about injecting code, you have to understand the two contexts in which a macro executes, or you risk generating code in the wrong place. One is the context of the macro definition, and the other is the caller's invocation of the macro. Let's see this in action by defining a definfo macro that prints a module's information in a friendly format while showing what context the code is executing in. Create a callers_context.exs file and type this in:

```
macros/callers_context.exs
Line 1  defmodule Mod do
  -       defmacro definfo do
  -         IO.puts "In macro's context (#{__MODULE__})."
  -
  5         quote do
  -           IO.puts "In caller's context (#{__MODULE__})."
  -
  -           def friendly_info do
  -             IO.puts """
  10            My name is #{__MODULE__}
  -             My functions are #{inspect __info__(:functions)}
  -             """
  -           end
  -         end
  15      end
  -     end
```

```
   defmodule MyModule do
     require Mod
20   Mod.definfo
   end
```

Now let's jump back to iex and load it:

```
iex> c "callers_context.exs"
In macro's context (Elixir.Mod).
In caller's context (Elixir.MyModule).
[MyModule, Mod]

iex> MyModule.friendly_info
My name is Elixir.MyModule
My functions are [friendly_info: 0]

:ok
```

We can see from the standard output that we entered both the macro and the caller's context when the module was compiled. Before the macro was expanded, we entered the definfo context on line 3. Next, our generated AST was expanded within the MyModule caller on line 6, where IO.puts was directly injected into the module body, along with the friendly_info function definition.

If you find yourself losing track of what context your code is executing in, it's often a sign that your code generation is too complex. You can avoid confusion by keeping macro definitions as short and straightforward as possible.

Hygiene Protects the Caller's Context

Elixir has the concept of macro *hygiene*. Hygiene means that variables, imports, and aliases that you define in a macro do not leak into the caller's own definitions. We must take special consideration with macro hygiene when expanding code, because sometimes it is a necessary evil to implicitly access the caller's scope in an unhygienic way.

When I first learned of hygiene, the name itself sounded very awkward and confusing—it wasn't a term I had heard before to describe code. But after an introduction, the idea of cleanliness and pollution-free execution really clicked. This safeguard not only prevents accidental namespace clashes, but also requires us to be explicit about reaching into the caller's context.

We've already seen how code injection works, but we haven't tried defining or accessing variables between different contexts. Let's explore a few examples to see how hygiene works. We'll use Code.eval_quoted again to evaluate an AST. Key in the following code block in iex:

```
iex> ast = quote do
...>    if meaning_to_life == 42 do
...>      "it's true"
...>    else
...>      "it remains to be seen"
...>    end
...> end
{:if, [context: Elixir, import: Kernel],
 [{:==, [context: Elixir, import: Kernel],
   [{:meaning_to_life, [], Elixir}, 42]},
  [do: "it's true", else: "it remains to be seen"]]}

iex> Code.eval_quoted ast, meaning_to_life: 42
** (CompileError) nofile:1: undefined function meaning_to_life/0
```

meaning_to_life wasn't available in the scope of our expression, even though it was passed as a binding to Code.eval_quoted. Elixir takes the safe approach of requiring you to explicitly allow a macro to define bindings in the caller's context. This design forces you to think about whether violating hygiene is necessary.

Overriding Hygiene

We can use the var! macro to explicitly override hygiene within a quoted expression. Let's re-create our previous iex session and use var! to reach into the caller's context:

```
iex> ast = quote do
...>    if var!(meaning_to_life) == 42 do
...>      "it's true"
...>    else
...>      "it remains to be seen"
...>    end
...> end
{:if, [context: Elixir, import: Kernel],
 [{:==, [context: Elixir, import: Kernel],
   [{:var!, [context: Elixir, import: Kernel],
     [{:meaning_to_life, [], Elixir}]}, 42]},
  [do: "it's true", else: "it remains to be seen"]]}

iex> Code.eval_quoted ast, meaning_to_life: 42
{"it's true", [meaning_to_life: 42]}

iex> Code.eval_quoted ast, meaning_to_life: 100
{"it remains to be seen", [meaning_to_life: 100]}
```

Let's try this out with macros by creating a module that can override a variable that has been previously defined by the caller. Key this into iex and follow along:

```
macros/setter1.exs
iex> defmodule Setter do
...>    defmacro bind_name(string) do
...>      quote do
...>        name = unquote(string)
...>      end
...>    end
...> end
{:module, Setter, ...

iex> require Setter
nil
iex> name = "Chris"
"Chris"
iex> Setter.bind_name("Max")
"Max"
iex> name
"Chris"
```

The name variable was not clobbered by the macro because hygiene protected the caller's scope. Again, we can use var! to allow our macro to produce an AST that has access to the caller's bindings when expanded:

```
macros/setter2.exs
iex> defmodule Setter do
...>    defmacro bind_name(string) do
...>      quote do
...>        var!(name) = unquote(string)
...>      end
...>    end
...> end
{:module, Setter, ...

iex> require Setter
nil
iex> name = "Chris"
"Chris"
iex> Setter.bind_name("Max")
"Max"
iex> name
"Max"
```

By using var!, we were able to override hygiene to rebind name to a new value. Overriding hygiene is useful on a case-by-case basis. Certain advanced use cases require overriding hygiene, but it should be avoided where possible because it can mask implementation details and add implicit behavior that is unknown to the caller. We'll selectively override hygiene in future exercises, but only where absolutely necessary.

When working with macros, it's important to be aware of what context a macro is executing in and to respect hygiene. We experimented with explicitly over-riding hygiene and explored the different contexts a macro enters throughout its lifecycle. We'll use these virtues to drive our implementations throughout the rest of this book.

Further Exploration

We've unlocked the secrets of the abstract syntax tree that underlies all the Elixir code you write. Through quoting expressions, manipulating ASTs, and defining macros, you're well on your way to advanced metaprogramming. In the coming chapter, we'll be building more advanced macros to create custom language constructs, and we'll write a mini testing framework that can infer meaning about Elixir expressions.

On your own, try expanding on the topics we covered. Here are a couple of ideas to get you started:

- Define an unless macro without depending on Kernel.if, by using other constructs in Elixir for control flow.
- Define a macro that returns a raw AST that you've written by hand, instead of using quote for code generation.

CHAPTER 2

Extending Elixir with Metaprogramming

Macros aren't just limited to the simple transformations you've done so far. They can be used to perform powerful code generation, save time, eliminate boilerplate, and produce elegant APIs. Once you realize that most of the Elixir standard library is implemented as macros, the possibilities really click about just how much freedom you have to extend the language. This can turn your language wish lists into immediate realities. Throughout this chapter, you'll find out how.

To continue our journey, we'll add brand-new control flow features to Elixir, extend the module system, and create a testing framework. Elixir puts all the building blocks of the language at our fingertips. It's time to start building.

Custom Language Constructs

You've seen that macros allow you to effectively create your own keywords in the language, but they also allow Elixir to be flexible against future requirements. For example, instead of waiting for the language to add a parallel `for` comprehension, you could extend the built-in `for` macro with a new `para` macro that spawns processes to run the comprehensions in parallel. It could look something like this:

```
para(for i <- 1..10 do: i * 10)
```

If implemented, `para` would transform the `for` AST into code that runs the comprehension in parallel. The original code would gain just one natural `para` invocation while executing the built-in comprehension in an entirely new way. José gave us a solid language foundation that we can craft to meet our needs.

Re-Creating the if Macro

Let's try out this idea. Consider the if macro from our unless example in the code on page 11. The if macro might appear special, but we know it's a macro like any other. Let's re-create Elixir's if macro to get a taste of how easy it is to implement features using the building blocks of the language.

Create an if_recreated.exs file and key this in:

```
macros/if_recreated.exs
defmodule ControlFlow do

  defmacro my_if(expr, do: if_block), do: if(expr, do: if_block, else: nil)
  defmacro my_if(expr, do: if_block, else: else_block) do
    quote do
      case unquote(expr) do
        result when result in [false, nil] -> unquote(else_block)
        _ -> unquote(if_block)
      end
    end
  end
end
```

Now, load it up in iex and test a couple of expressions:

```
iex> c "if_recreated.exs"
[MyIf]

iex> require ControlFlow
nil
iex> ControlFlow.my_if 1 == 1 do
...>   "correct"
...> else
...>   "incorrect"
...> end
"correct"
```

In fewer than ten lines of code, we re-created an essential construct in Elixir using case to handle control flow.

Now that you've had a taste of first-class macros, let's make things more interesting by creating an entirely new language feature. We'll use this same technique where existing macros will serve as building blocks of our implementation.

Adding a while Loop to Elixir

You may have noticed that Elixir lacks the familiar while loop that is found in most languages. It's not an essential feature, but sometimes it would be convenient to have around. If you find yourself longing for missing features, remember that Elixir was designed to be extensible. The language is small because it doesn't have to include all common features. If we need a while loop, we have all the power to create it. Let's make it happen.

We'll extend Elixir with a new while macro that loops repeatedly with the ability to break out of its own execution. Here's an example of the feature we're going to create:

```
while Process.alive?(pid) do
  send pid, {self, :ping}
  receive do
    {^pid, :pong} -> IO.puts "Got pong"
  after 2000 -> break
  end
end
```

When creating a feature like this, it's best to start by choosing which Elixir building blocks will be required to accomplish your high-level goals. Our main issue is that Elixir has no built-in way to loop infinitely. So how are we to handle a repetitive loop without such a feature? We cheat. We can get creative by consuming an infinite stream with for to achieve the same effect as an infinite loop.

Head back to your editor and create a while.exs file. We'll start by defining a while macro within a Loop module:

macros/while_step1.exs
```
defmodule Loop do

  defmacro while(expression, do: block) do
    quote do
      for _ <- Stream.cycle([:ok]) do
        if unquote(expression) do
          unquote(block)
        else
          # break out of loop
        end
      end
    end
  end
end
```

We began by pattern matching directly on the provided expression and block of code. Like all macros, we need to produce an AST for the caller, so we started a quoted expression. Next, we effectively created an infinite loop by consuming the infinite stream, Stream.cycle([:ok]). Within our for block, we injected the expression into an if/else clause to conditionally execute the provided block of code. We haven't yet provided a way to break out of execution, but let's experiment with our infinite loop in iex to make sure we're on the right track.

Go ahead and execute your file in iex, but be ready to trigger Control-C to break out of the infinite loop we've created:

```
iex(1)> c "while.exs"
[Loop]
iex(2)> import Loop
nil
iex(3)> while true do
...(3)>   IO.puts "looping!"
...(3)> end
looping!
looping!
looping!
looping!
looping!
looping!
...
^C^C
```

Our first step is complete. We were able to repeatedly execute a block of code given an expression. Now we need the ability to break out of execution once the expression is no longer true. Elixir's for comprehension has no built-in way to terminate early, but with a careful try/catch block, we can throw a value to stop execution. Let's throw and catch a :break value to halt the infinite loop.

Update your Loop module with the following code:

```
macros/while_step2.exs
Line 1  defmodule Loop do

        defmacro while(expression, do: block) do
          quote do
    5         try do
              for _ <- Stream.cycle([:ok]) do
                if unquote(expression) do
                  unquote(block)
                else
   10               throw :break
                end
              end
            catch
              :break -> :ok
   15         end
          end
        end
  -   end
```

On line 5, we wrapped our entire for comprehension within a try/catch block. Next, we simply threw a :break value on line 10 and caught the value on line 14 to break out of the infinite loop. Let's see it in action in iex:

```
iex> c "while.exs"
[Loop]
iex> import Loop

iex> run_loop = fn ->
...>   pid = spawn(fn -> :timer.sleep(4000) end)
...>   while Process.alive?(pid) do
...>     IO.puts "#{inspect :erlang.time} Stayin' alive!"
...>     :timer.sleep 1000
...>   end
...> end
#Function<20.90072148/0 in :erl_eval.expr/5>

iex> run_loop.()
{8, 11, 15} Stayin' alive!
{8, 11, 16} Stayin' alive!
{8, 11, 17} Stayin' alive!
{8, 11, 18} Stayin' alive!
:ok
iex>
```

We now have a functioning while loop. Careful use of throw allows us to break out of execution whenever the while expression is no longer true. Let's provide a break function to allow the caller to explicitly terminate execution:

```
macros/while.exs
Line 1  defmodule Loop do

        defmacro while(expression, do: block) do
          quote do
    5       try do
              for _ <- Stream.cycle([:ok]) do
                if unquote(expression) do
                  unquote(block)
                else
    10            Loop.break
                end
              end
            catch
              :break -> :ok
    15      end
          end
        end

        def break, do: throw :break
    20 end
```

On line 19, we defined a break function for the caller that throws the :break value. The caller could throw the value, but providing a high-level break function abstracts the internal implementation and unifies the termination with the while macro. Let's head over to iex to experiment with our final implementation:

```
iex> c "while.exs"
[Loop]

iex> import Loop
nil

iex>
pid = spawn fn ->
  while true do
    receive do
      :stop ->
        IO.puts "Stopping..."
        break
      message ->
        IO.puts "Got #{inspect message}"
    end
  end
end
#PID<0.93.0>

iex> send pid, :hello
Got :hello
:hello

iex> send pid, :ping
Got :ping
:ping

iex> send pid, :stop
Stopping...
:stop

iex> Process.alive? pid
false
```

We've created an entirely new addition to the language! We used the same technique that Elixir uses internally by leveraging existing macros as building blocks. Step by step, we transformed the expression and code block into an infinite loop with conditional termination.

This kind of extension is what Elixir is all about. Next, we'll use AST introspection for smarter assertions and create a mini testing framework.

Smarter Testing with Macros

If you're familiar with writing tests in most mainstream languages, you know it can take a while to learn the different assertion functions of testing frameworks. For example, let's see how a few basic assertions for popular test frameworks in Ruby and JavaScript compare to Elixir. You don't need to be familiar with these languages; just be mindful of the different assertion APIs.

JavaScript:

```
expect(value).toBe(true);
expect(value).toEqual(12);
expect(value).toBeGreaterThan(100);
```

Ruby:

```
assert value
assert_equal value, 12
assert_operator value, :<=, 100
```

Elixir:

```
assert value
assert value == 12
assert value <= 100
```

Notice how such simple assertions took on arbitrary method and function names in Ruby and JavaScript? They might read nicely, but they subtly mask the expression being tested. They also require a new mental model for each test framework on how assertions should be made for the given expression.

The reason these languages require methods and functions like this is to ensure relevant failure messages. If an assertion like assert value <= 100 failed in Ruby, you would only receive a less than helpful "expected true, got false" test output. By providing unique functions per assertion, the correct failure messages can be generated, but it comes at a cost of a larger testing API. You also take on the mental overhead of which function is required each time you need to write an assertion. There's a better way.

Macros power Elixir's ExUnit test framework. As you've seen, they give you access to the internal representation of any Elixir expression. This allows a single assert macro to peer into the code representation to provide contextual failure messages. With macros, we can sidestep the arbitrary functions and assertion rules from other languages because we have access to the meaning of each expression. We'll be taking full advantage of Elixir to write a smart assert macro and create a mini testing framework.

Supercharged Assertions

The goal for our assert macro is to accept a left-hand side and right-hand side expression, separated by an Elixir operator, such as assert 1 > 0. If an assertion fails, we'll print a helpful failure message based on the expression being tested. Our macro will peek inside the representation of the assertions in order to print the correct test output.

Here's a high-level example of what we want to accomplish:

```
defmodule Test do
  import Assertion
  def run
    assert 5 == 5
    assert 2 > 0
    assert 10 < 1
  end
end

iex> Test.run
..
FAILURE:
  Expected: 10
  to be less than: 1
```

As always, we'll start small by experimenting in iex with a few example expressions that our macro will accept:

```
iex> quote do: 5 == 5
{:==, [context: Elixir, import: Kernel], [5, 5]}

iex> quote do: 2 < 10
{:<, [context: Elixir, import: Kernel], [2, 10]}
```

A simple numerical comparison yields a straightforward AST. We received the operator as an atom, representing the Kernel function call to perform, and the left-hand side and right-hand side values are contained in the list of arguments. Using this representation, we have everything we need to begin our assert implementation.

Create an assertion.exs file and add the following code to it:

```
macros/assert_step1.exs
defmodule Assertion do

  # {:==, [context: Elixir, import: Kernel], [5, 5]}
  defmacro assert({operator, _, [lhs, rhs]}) do
    quote bind_quoted: [operator: operator, lhs: lhs, rhs: rhs] do
      Assertion.Test.assert(operator, lhs, rhs)
    end
```

```
    end
end
```

We began by pattern matching directly on the provided AST expression, using our iex examples to drive our argument match. Next, we generated a single line of code using our pattern-matched bindings that simply proxies to an Assertion.Test.assert function that we'll write in a moment. Here, we also used bind_quoted for the first time. Before we continue our assert macro, let's take a detour to see what bind_quoted is all about.

bind_quoted

The quote macro's bind_quoted option passes a binding to the block, ensuring that the outside bound variables are unquoted only a single time. We could have written our quote block without bind_quoted, but it's good practice to use it whenever possible to prevent accidental reevaluation of bindings. For example, the following blocks of code are equivalent:

```
quote bind_quoted: [operator: operator, lhs: lhs, rhs: rhs] do
  Assertion.Test.assert(operator, lhs, rhs)
end
```

```
quote do
  Assertion.Test.assert(unquote(operator), unquote(lhs), unquote(rhs))
end
```

Using bind_quoted here doesn't gain us much, but let's imagine a different example to see why using it is good practice. Imagine if we built our own Debugger.log macro that executes an expression but calls IO.inspect on the results only when in debug mode.

Key in this code and save it as debugger.exs:

```
macros/debugger.exs
Line 1  defmodule Debugger do
   -      defmacro log(expression) do
   -        if Application.get_env(:debugger, :log_level) == :debug do
   -          quote do
   5            IO.puts "=================="
   -            IO.inspect unquote(expression)
   -            IO.puts "=================="
   -            unquote(expression)
   -          end
   10         else
   -           expression
   -        end
   -      end
   -  end
```

We defined a simple Debugger.log macro that accepts an expression. If the configured :log_level at compile time is :debug, we print a debug output of the expression on line 6. After printing, we execute the expression as normal on line 8. Let's see the issue with this setup by running the code in iex:

```
iex> c "debugger.exs"
[Debugger]

iex> require Debugger
nil

iex> Application.put_env(:debugger, :log_level, :debug)
:ok

iex> remote_api_call = fn -> IO.puts("calling remote API...") end
#Function<20.90072148/0 in :erl_eval.expr/5>

iex> Debugger.log(remote_api_call.())
==================
calling remote API...
:ok
==================
calling remote API...
:ok
iex>
```

The remote_api_call.() expression was invoked twice! This is because we accidentally unquoted the expression twice in our log macro. Let's fix this by using bind_quoted.

Update your debugger.exs with the following code:

```
macros/debugger_fixed.exs
defmodule Debugger do
  defmacro log(expression) do
    if Application.get_env(:debugger, :log_level) == :debug do
      quote bind_quoted: [expression: expression] do
        IO.puts "=================="
        IO.inspect expression
        IO.puts "=================="
        expression
      end
    else
      expression
    end
  end
end
```

We updated our quote block to use bind_quoted so that expression is unquoted and bound to a variable a single time. Now let's try it again in iex:

```
iex> c "debugger_fixed.exs"
[Debugger]

iex> Debugger.log(remote_api_call.())
calling remote API...
=================
:ok
=================
:ok
iex>
```

Our function call is now executed only a single time. Using bind_quoted will keep you safe from accidental reevaluations. It also cleans up your quote blocks since you don't have to use unquote for every injected binding. One thing to keep in mind when using bind_quoted is that unquote is disabled. You won't be able to use the unquote macro unless you explicitly pass the unquote: true option to quote. Now that we know how bind_quoted works, let's continue our Assertion framework.

Leveraging the VM's Pattern Matching Engine

Now that our assert macro is in place, we can implement the proxy assert functions in a new Assertion.Test module. The Assertion.Test module will carry out the work of performing the assertions and running our tests. When you find yourself at a stage in code where you've proxied out to a function that you are about to implement, try to think about how pattern matching can help guide your implementation. Let's see how to make the Virtual Machine do as much work for us as possible while helping to keep our code clear and concise.

Update your assertion.exs file with the following code:

```
macros/assert_step2.exs
Line 1 defmodule Assertion do

         defmacro assert({operator, _, [lhs, rhs]}) do
           quote bind_quoted: [operator: operator, lhs: lhs, rhs: rhs] do
    5          Assertion.Test.assert(operator, lhs, rhs)
           end
         end
       end

   10 defmodule Assertion.Test do
         def assert(:==, lhs, rhs) when lhs == rhs do
           IO.write "."
         end
         def assert(:==, lhs, rhs) do
   15      IO.puts """
         FAILURE:
```

```
-         Expected:        #{lhs}
-         to be equal to: #{rhs}
-       """
20    end
-
-     def assert(:>, lhs, rhs) when lhs > rhs do
-       IO.write "."
-     end
25    def assert(:>, lhs, rhs) do
-       IO.puts """
-       FAILURE:
-         Expected:           #{lhs}
-         to be greater than: #{rhs}
30      """
-     end
- end
```

By generating a single line of code on line 5 to proxy to Assertion.Test.assert, we let the Virtual Machine's pattern matching take over to report the result of each assertion. We also placed the functions under a new Test module so our Assertion imports won't leak into the caller's module. We only want the caller to import the Assertion macros, so we delegate out to another module to avoid importing unnecessary functions.

This also highlights an effective approach to macros, where the goal is to generate as little code as possible within the caller's context. By proxying to an outside function, we keep the code generation as straightforward as possible. As you'll see later, this approach is pivotal to writing maintainable macros.

To make some assertions, we simply need to write an Assertion.Test.assert definition for each operator in Elixir and display the relevant failure messages. First, let's explore our current implementation in iex. Go ahead and try out a few assertions of your own:

```
iex> c "assertion.exs"
[Assertion.Test, Assertion]

iex> import Assertion
nil

iex> assert 1 > 2
FAILURE:
  Expected:           1
  to be greater than: 2

:ok

iex> assert 5 == 5
.:ok
```

```
iex> assert 10 * 10 == 100
.:ok
```

To make running our tests more convenient, let's add a quick MathTest module to run some assertions and simulate a module being tested:

```
macros/math_test_import.exs
defmodule MathTest do
  import Assertion

  def run do
    assert 5 == 5
    assert 10 > 0
    assert 1 > 2
    assert 10 * 10 == 100
  end
end

iex> MathTest.run
..FAILURE:
  Expected:           1
  to be greater than: 2

.:ok
```

The beginnings of a test framework are steadily taking shape, but there's a problem with our implementation. Forcing users to implement their own run/0 function isn't terribly convenient. It would also be nice to provide a way to group test cases by name or description.

Next, we will expand on our simple assert macro, creating the beginnings of a testing DSL. Domain-specific languages are covered extensively in Chapter 5, *Creating an HTML Domain-Specific Language*, on page 75, and this is just our first taste.

Extending Modules

A core purpose of macros is to inject code into modules to extend their behavior, define functions, and perform any other code generation that's required. For our Assertion framework, our goal is to extend other modules with a test macro. The macro will accept a test-case description as a string, followed by a block of code where assertions can be made. Failure messages will be prefixed by the description to help debug the failing test cases. We'll also define the run/0 function automatically for the caller so that all test cases can be executed by a single function call.

Our goal throughout this section is to produce the following testing DSL, which extends any module with our mini testing framework. Take a look at this code, but don't worry about keying it in just yet:

```
Line 1  defmodule MathTest do
          use Assertion

          test "integers can be added and subtracted" do
     5      assert 1 + 1 == 2
            assert 2 + 3 == 5
            assert 5 - 5 == 10
          end

    10    test "integers can be multiplied and divided" do
            assert 5 * 5 == 25
            assert 10 / 2 == 5
          end
        end
    15
        iex> MathTest.run
        ..
        ================================================
        FAILURE: integers can be added and subtracted
    20  ================================================
          Expected:       0
          to be equal to: 10
        ..:ok
```

On line 2, we see use for the first time. We'll talk more about that in a moment. To achieve our testing goals, we need to provide a way for our Assertion module to generate a bit of code within the caller's context. In our case, we need to define a run/0 function automatically for users, within their module's context, that performs the test-case evaluation. Let's get to work.

Module Extension Is Simply Code Injection

Most metaprogramming in Elixir is done within module definitions to extend other modules with extra functionality. We briefly experimented with module extension in *Code Injection and the Caller's Context*, on page 16; now let's see what it's all about.

Let's explore how we can extend modules by using only the tools you've learned so far. In the process, you'll get a better understanding of how Elixir module extension works internally.

Let's write an extend macro that can inject our stubbed run/0 definition in the context of another module. Create a module_extension_custom.exs file and follow along in your editor:

```
                    macros/module_extension_custom.exs
Line 1  defmodule Assertion do
    -     # ...
    -     defmacro extend(options \\ []) do
    -       quote do
    5         import unquote(__MODULE__)

    -         def run do
    -           IO.puts "Running the tests..."
    -         end
    10      end
    -     end
    -     # ...
    -   end

    -
    15  defmodule MathTest do
    -     require Assertion
    -     Assertion.extend
    -   end
```

Now run the code in iex:

```
iex> c "module_extension_custom.exs"
[MathTest]

iex> MathTest.run
Running the tests...
:ok
```

On line 3, we were able to inject a stubbed run/0 function directly into the MathTest module via our Assertion.extend macro. Assertion.extend is just a regular macro that returned an AST containing the run/0 definition. This example underlines the building-block nature of Elixir's code construction. With no other mechanism than defmacro and quote, we defined a function within another module!

use: A Common API for Module Extension

One reoccurring theme that you may have noticed in many Elixir libraries is the prevalence of the use SomeModule syntax. You have probably typed it many times in your own projects without fully understanding what it does. The use macro serves the simple but powerful purpose of providing a common API for module extension. use SomeModule simply invokes the SomeModule.__using__/1 macro. By providing a common API for extension, this little macro will be the center of the metaprogramming we'll perform throughout the rest of this book.

Let's rewrite the previous example with use to take advantage of Elixir's common extension API. Update your module_extension_custom.exs file with the following code:

```
macros/module_extension_use.exs
Line 1  defmodule Assertion do
   -      # ...
   -      defmacro __using__(_options) do
   -        quote do
   5          import unquote(__MODULE__)
   -
   -          def run do
   -            IO.puts "Running the tests..."
   -          end
   10       end
   -      end
   -      # ...
   -    end
   -
   15  defmodule MathTest do
   -      use Assertion
   -    end
```

Now let's try it out:

```
iex> MathTest.run
Running the tests...
:ok
```

On lines 3 and 16, we leveraged use and __using__ to extend the MathTest module with Elixir's common API. The result is identical to our original Assertion.extend example, but staying within Elixir's common API is idiomatic and flexible to future changes.

The neat thing about the use macro is that it feels like an untouchable keyword, but in reality it's just a macro that does a bit of code injection like our own extend definition. The fact that use is just a regular macro really shows off how true Elixir stays to being a small language built by macros. With our run/0 stub in place, we're ready to move on to the test macro.

Using Module Attributes for Code Generation

Before we can implement the test macro, we need to address a missing piece to our implementation. A user can define multiple test cases, but we have no way of tracking each test-case definition for inclusion within MathTest.run/0. Fortunately, Elixir solves this use case via module attributes.

Module attributes allow data to be stored in the module at compile time. They are often used in places where constants would be applied in other languages, but Elixir provides other tricks for us to exploit during compilation. By taking advantage of the accumulate: true option when registering an attribute, we can keep an appended list of registrations during the compile phase. After the module is compiled, the attribute contains a list of all registrations that occurred during compilation. Let's see how this can be used for our test macro.

Our test macro will accept two arguments: a string description followed by a keyword list for the do/end code block. Add this latest code to the top of your original Assertion module within assertion.exs:

```
macros/accumulated_module_attributes.exs
defmodule Assertion do

  defmacro __using__(_options) do
    quote do
      import unquote(__MODULE__)
      Module.register_attribute __MODULE__, :tests, accumulate: true
      def run do
        IO.puts "Running the tests (#{inspect @tests})"
      end
    end
  end

  defmacro test(description, do: test_block) do
    test_func = String.to_atom(description)
    quote do
      @tests {unquote(test_func), unquote(description)}
      def unquote(test_func)(), do: unquote(test_block)
    end
  end
  # ...
end
```

On line 6, we registered a tests attribute with the accumulate option set to true. On line 8, we inspected the @tests attribute in our stubbed run/0 function. Next, we defined a test macro, which first converts the test-case description to an atom so that it can serve as a valid function name. On lines 15 through 18, we closed the macro by generating a couple of lines of code within the caller's context. First, we accumulated the test_func reference and description in the @tests module attribute.

We finished by defining a function whose name was the description converted to an atom, and whose function body was everything contained in the do/end block of the test case. The result of our new macro leaves the caller with an accumulated list of test metadata, as well as defined functions to perform the test-case evaluation.

Let's try our new implementation. Create a math_test_step1.exs module with the following code:

```
macros/math_test_step1.exs
defmodule MathTest do
  use Assertion

  test "integers can be added and subtracted" do
    assert 1 + 1 == 2
    assert 2 + 3 == 5
    assert 5 - 5 == 10
  end
end
```

Now let's run it in iex:

```
iex> c "assertion.exs"
[Assertion.Test, Assertion]

iex> c "math_test_step1.exs"
[MathTest]

iex> MathTest.__info__(:functions)
["integers can be added and subtracted": 0, run: 0]

iex> MathTest.run
Running the tests ([])
:ok
```

What happened? It appears our @tests module attribute is empty, even though it was properly accumulated in the test macro. If we re-examine the __using__ block of our Assertion module, we can see the issue:

```
defmacro __using__(_options) do
  quote do
    import unquote(__MODULE__)
    Module.register_attribute __MODULE__, :tests, accumulate: true
    def run do
      IO.puts "Running the tests (#{inspect @tests})"
    end
  end
end
```

The location of run/0 reveals the problem. We defined it just after registering the tests attribute. The run function definition was expanded within the MathTest module at our use Assertion declaration. The result is that run/0 was expanded in MathTest before any of the test macro accumulations were registered. We need a way to delay macro expansion until after we've done some code-generation work. Elixir provides a before_compile hook for this purpose.

Compile-Time Hooks

Elixir allows us to set a special module attribute, @before_compile, to notify the compiler that an extra step is required just before compilation is finished. The @before_compile attribute accepts a module argument where a __before_compile__/1 macro must be defined. This macro is invoked just before compilation in order to perform a final bit of code generation. Let's apply this hook to fix our test macro. Update your Assertion module with these @before_compile hooks:

```
macros/before_compile.exs
Line 1  defmodule Assertion do

          defmacro __using__(_options) do
            quote do
    5         import unquote(__MODULE__)
              Module.register_attribute __MODULE__, :tests, accumulate: true
              @before_compile unquote(__MODULE__)
            end
          end
   10
          defmacro __before_compile__(_env) do
            quote do
              def run do
                IO.puts "Running the tests (#{inspect @tests})"
   15         end
            end
          end

          defmacro test(description, do: test_block) do
   20       test_func = String.to_atom(description)
            quote do
              @tests {unquote(test_func), unquote(description)}
              def unquote(test_func)(), do: unquote(test_block)
            end
   25     end
          # ...
        end
```

Now let's test in iex:

```
iex> c "assertion.exs"
[Assertion.Test, Assertion]

iex> c "math_test_step1.exs"
[MathTest]
```

```
iex> MathTest.run
Running the tests (["integers can be added and subtracted":
"integers can be added and subtracted"])
:ok
```

It works! On line 7, we registered a before_compile attribute hook to have Assert.__before_compile__/1 invoked just before MathTest is finished being compiled. This allows our accumulated @tests attribute on line 14 to expand properly because it was defined after the test-case registrations.

To complete our framework, we now need to implement the run/0 definition to enumerate all test cases accumulated in @tests and invoke each test function. Here's the final code listing with the new run/0 definition. Let's look at how all of the parts fit together:

macros/assertion.exs
```elixir
Line 1  defmodule Assertion do

          defmacro __using__(_options) do
            quote do
    5         import unquote(__MODULE__)
              Module.register_attribute __MODULE__, :tests, accumulate: true
              @before_compile unquote(__MODULE__)
            end
          end
    10
          defmacro __before_compile__(_env) do
            quote do
              def run, do: Assertion.Test.run(@tests, __MODULE__)
            end
    15    end

          defmacro test(description, do: test_block) do
            test_func = String.to_atom(description)
            quote do
    20        @tests {unquote(test_func), unquote(description)}
              def unquote(test_func)(), do: unquote(test_block)
            end
          end

    25    defmacro assert({operator, _, [lhs, rhs]}) do
            quote bind_quoted: [operator: operator, lhs: lhs, rhs: rhs] do
              Assertion.Test.assert(operator, lhs, rhs)
            end
          end
    30  end

        defmodule Assertion.Test do
          def run(tests, module) do
            Enum.each tests, fn {test_func, description} ->
```

```
35      case apply(module, test_func, []) do
          :ok             -> IO.write "."
          {:fail, reason} -> IO.puts """

          ===============================================
40        FAILURE: #{description}
          ===============================================
          #{reason}
          """
        end
45    end
    end

    def assert(:==, lhs, rhs) when lhs == rhs do
      :ok
50    end
    def assert(:==, lhs, rhs) do
      {:fail, """
        Expected:       #{lhs}
        to be equal to: #{rhs}
55      """
      }
    end

    def assert(:>, lhs, rhs) when lhs > rhs do
60    :ok
    end
    def assert(:>, lhs, rhs) do
      {:fail, """
        Expected:          #{lhs}
65      to be greater than: #{rhs}
        """
      }
    end
  end
```

On line 13, we generated run/0 within the using module's context, waiting until just before compilation is complete so that our @tests module attribute contains all the accumulated test metadata. It simply proxies to our Assertion.Test.run/2 function defined on lines 33–46. We refactored our Assertion.Test.assert definitions to return either :ok or {:fail, reason} instead of printing the assertion results directly. This allows our run function to report the test results accordingly and opens up more flexible reporting for future extension. Continuing a trend we first saw with the original assert macro, our run/0 definition proxies to an outside function to generate as little code as possible within the caller's context. Let's see it in action:

```
macros/math_test_final.exs
defmodule MathTest do
  use Assertion
  test "integers can be added and subtracted" do
    assert 2 + 3 == 5
    assert 5 - 5 == 10
  end
  test "integers can be multiplied and divided" do
    assert 5 * 5 == 25
    assert 10 / 2 == 5
  end
end

iex> MathTest.run

.

===================================================
FAILURE: integers can be added and subtracted
===================================================
Expected:      0
to be equal to: 10
```

We've created a mini testing framework, complete with its own pattern-matching definitions, testing DSL, and compile-time hooks for advanced code generation. Most importantly, we generated code responsibly: our macro expansions are concise and we delegated to outside functions where possible to keep our code easy to reason about. If you're wondering how to test macros themselves, we'll cover testing in Chapter 4, *How to Test Macros*, on page 65.

Further Exploration

We journeyed from simple control flow transformations all the way through a mini testing framework. Along the way, you learned all the tools necessary to define your own macros and perform AST transformations in a responsible way. Next, we'll discover a few advanced compile-time code-generation techniques to create highly performant and maintainable programs.

On your own, explore ways you can enhance your Assertion test framework and define new macro constructs. Here are a few basic experiments to get you started:

- Implement assert for every operator in Elixir.
- Add Boolean assertions, such as assert true.
- Implement a refute macro for refutations.

And some that are more advanced:

- Run test cases in parallel within Assertion.Test.run/2 via spawned processes.
- Add reports for the module. Include pass/fail counts and execution time.

CHAPTER 3

Advanced Compile-Time Code Generation

So far we've performed compile-time code generation through careful use of macros. Now let's shift gears and exploit Elixir's module system. With advanced metaprogramming, we can embed data and behavior within modules directly from outside sources of information. This technique can remove countless lines of boilerplate, while producing highly optimized programs. We'll start by exploring how Elixir embeds an entire unicode database at compile time for its robust Unicode support. Next, we'll build MIME-type validation and internationalization libraries, while applying compile-time optimizations that aren't possible in many languages. Knowing when and where to use this technique will allow us to construct fast, maintainable programs in strikingly few lines of code.

Generating Functions from External Data

Turning raw data into code might sound impractical, but it's an extremely nice solution to a number of problems. Ever wonder how Elixir manages its fantastic String Unicode support? The way it goes about it is my favorite metaprogramming example to date. The String.Unicode module of the standard library dynamically generates thousands of function definitions from external data when compiled. These generated functions pattern match on all known Unicode characters to achieve the best Unicode support in languages today. Let's look inside the String.Unicode module to understand how Elixir makes this happen.

Instead of manually mapping tens of thousands of Unicode code points into an Elixir data structure, a UnicodeData.txt file is checked into the Elixir source repository, which contains every known Unicode code-point mapping. This dataset is read in at compile time to produce function definitions that handle Unicode conversions. Here's an overview of how it works:

UnicodeData.txt snippet:

```
...
00C7;LATIN CAPITAL LETTER C WITH CEDILLA;Lu;0;L;0043 0327;...
00C8;LATIN CAPITAL LETTER E WITH GRAVE;Lu;0;L;0045 0300;...
00C9;LATIN CAPITAL LETTER E WITH ACUTE;Lu;0;L;0045 0301;...
00CA;LATIN CAPITAL LETTER E WITH CIRCUMFLEX;Lu;0;L;0045 0302;...
00CB;LATIN CAPITAL LETTER E WITH DIAERESIS;Lu;0;L;0045 0308;...
...
```

The UnicodeData.txt file contains 27,000 lines of these semicolon-delimited code-point mappings. The String.Unicode module opens the file at compile time and parses the code points into function definitions. The final expansion contains a function definition per code point for case conversions and other string transformations. Let's take a look at what the cross-section of String.Unicode would look like after its functions have been generated. It should give you a sense of how generating functions from data files opens up unique pattern-matching possibilities.

```elixir
defmodule String.Unicode do
  ...
  def upcase(string), do: do_upcase(string) |> IO.iodata_to_binary
  ...
  defp do_upcase("é" <> rest) do
    :binary.bin_to_list("É") ++ do_upcase(rest)
  end
  defp do_upcase("ć" <> rest) do
    :binary.bin_to_list("Ć") ++ do_upcase(rest)
  end
  defp do_upcase("ü" <> rest) do
    :binary.bin_to_list("Ü") ++ do_upcase(rest)
  end
  ...
  defp do_upcase(char <> rest) do
    :binary.bin_to_list(char) ++ do_upcase(rest)
  end
  ...
end
```

The compiled module contains thousands of these definitions! When converting a string like "Thanks José!" to uppercase, String.Unicode simply calls do_upcase/1 recursively for each code point in the string. When "é" is encountered, the generated function for that code point is matched and returns the uppercase version. It's an extremely elegant solution to an otherwise difficult problem. Let's break it down to see how the algorithm works.

upcase("José")

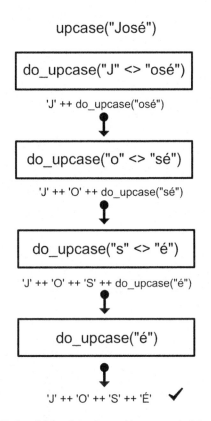

By using the Erlang Virtual Machine's pattern-matching engine, Elixir gains performant string manipulation in a fraction of the code that would need to be written by hand. The beauty of this technique is that new unicode characters can be supported in the future by updating UnicodeData.txt and running mix compile.

Now that you've had a glimpse of the way Elixir takes advantage of code generation from external data, let's apply this technique to our own MIME-type and internationalization libraries.

MIME-Type Conversion in Ten Lines of Code

If you've ever written a web service, you've probably needed to validate and convert MIME types to their file extension. For example, when a request comes into the server with an Accept header of application/javascript, we must know how to handle this MIME type and render a .js template. To tackle this problem in most languages, we would store the MIME data in a map and consult the keyspace for MIME-type conversions. This can become tedious with large datasets where we would need to convert the data by hand into a format representable within our programs. Fortunately, Elixir makes this easy for us with just a touch of metaprogramming. Head back over to your editor and let's get to work.

Making Use of Existing Datasets

We'll accomplish our MIME library goals by working smarter, not harder. Instead of writing a bunch of code by hand, we'll take a publicly available MIME-type dataset and generate function heads to perform conversions. Our solution will require only ten lines of code, while remaining fast and maintainable.

We first need to find a MIME-type dataset to serve as the basis of our implementation. Luckily, a quick Internet search turns up a nicely formatted, extensive MIME-type text file.[1] Let's take a look at the first five lines of the file to get an idea of how we can parse it into function definitions. Go ahead and copy the full mimes.txt file to your own computer:

advanced_code_gen/mimes.txt
```
application/javascript   .js
application/json          .json
image/jpeg       .jpeg, .jpg
video/jpeg       .jpgv
```

The full mimes.txt contains 685 lines that map standard MIME types to their file extensions. To parse this file, we can split each line by tab and comma to obtain the MIME type and file extensions. Let's define a Mime module to perform the conversions using the mimes.txt file we just created.

Create a mime.exs file and add this code to it. Be sure your mimes.txt file is located in the same directory.

advanced_code_gen/mime.exs
```
Line 1  defmodule Mime do
          for line <- File.stream!(Path.join([__DIR__, "mimes.txt"]), [], :line) do
            [type, rest] = line |> String.split("\t") |> Enum.map(&String.strip(&1))
            extensions = String.split(rest, ~r/,\s?/)
     5
            def exts_from_type(unquote(type)), do: unquote(extensions)
            def type_from_ext(ext) when ext in unquote(extensions), do: unquote(type)
          end

    10    def exts_from_type(_type), do: []
          def type_from_ext(_ext), do: nil
          def valid_type?(type), do: exts_from_type(type) |> Enum.any?
        end
```

---

1.   http://www.iana.org/assignments/media-types/media-types.xhtml

In ten lines of code, we created an entire MIME-type conversion and validation module! On line 2, we read the mimes.txt file line by line and split the MIME type and file extensions from each. For each line, we defined two functions—one for mapping MIME type to file extension, and the other for mapping file extension to MIME type. We used the standard def macro to define each function and unquote to inject our MIME and file extension values. To complete the module, we defined catch-all clauses for exts_from_type and type_from_ext. These provide a guaranteed fallback if the generated definitions fail to match. We finished by defining a valid_type? function that simply delegates to prior definitions. Let's test our generated functions in iex:

```
Line 1   iex> c "mime.exs"
    -    [Mime]
    -
    -    iex> Mime.exts_from_type("image/jpeg")
    5    [".jpeg", ".jpg"]
    -
    -    iex> Mime.type_from_ext(".jpg")
    -    "image/jpeg"
    -
   10    iex> Mime.valid_type?("text/html")
    -    true
    -
    -    iex> Mime.valid_type?("text/emoji")
    -    false
```

On lines 4 and 7, we confirmed that our generated functions properly convert MIME type to file extensions and vice versa. We can also see that our valid_type? functions correctly validate known MIME types. You might be wondering how we were able to call unquote outside of a quote block when defining our generated functions. Elixir supports the idea of *unquote fragments*. Unquote fragments allow you to create functions dynamically, like we did in our for comprehension above.

```
def exts_from_type(unquote(type)), do: unquote(extensions)
def type_from_ext(ext) when ext in unquote(extensions), do: unquote(type)
```

We used unquote fragments to define multiple heads of the exts_from_type and type_from_ext functions, but we can also use them to define function names on the fly. Consider this block of code:

```
iex> defmodule Fragments do
...>   for {name, val} <- [one: 1, two: 2, three: 3] do
...>     def unquote(name)(), do: unquote(val)
...>   end
...> end
{:module, Fragments, ...
```

```
iex> Fragments.one
1

iex> Fragments.two
2
```

With unquote fragments, we can pass any valid atom to def and dynamically define a function with that name. We'll use unquote fragments heavily throughout the rest of this chapter.

Some of the most enjoyable solutions are the ones that are almost unbelievable the first time you see them. Using a tiny amount of code, we built for any web service an essential tool that is fast and maintainable. Future MIME-type support requires only a small edit to mimes.txt. Fewer lines of code mean fewer bugs, code paths, and failure scenarios. Defining multiple function heads leverages the VM's pattern-matching prowess to do the heavy lifting for us.

Next, we'll expand on this technique by defining an internationalization library. But first, there's one more issue.

Recompiling Modules when External Resources Change

Our Mime module works great, but if we modify the mimes.txt file, our module won't be automatically recompiled by mix, Elixir's build tool.[2] This is because the source file did not change. Elixir provides the @external_resource module attribute to handle cases where we want to specify compile-time resources that our module depends on—when the resources change, mix will recompile our module. Let's register an @external_resource attribute in our Mime module to fix this issue.

advanced_code_gen/external_resource.exs
```elixir
defmodule Mime do

  @external_resource mimes_path = Path.join([__DIR__, "mimes.txt"])

  for line <- File.stream!(mimes_path, [], :line) do
    # ...
end
```

Now when mimes.txt changes, mix will automatically recompile our Mime module. The @external_resource is an accumulated attribute, so any number of resources can be registered on a single module. Use @external_resource any time your module depends on a non-source file for its body definition. It will save you time and frustration by properly recompiling dynamically generated modules.

---

2.   http://elixir-lang.org/getting_started/mix_otp/1.html

Building an Internationalization Library

Almost all user-facing applications are best served by an internationalization layer where language snippets can be stored and referenced programmatically. Let's use code generation to produce an internationalization library in fewer lines of code than you thought possible. This is the most advanced exercise you've done so far, so let's start by breaking down our implementation into a rubric that you can use to attack complex metaprogramming problems.

Step 1: Plan Your Macro API

The first step of our Translator implementation is to plan the surface area of our macro API. This is often called README Driven Development. It helps tease out our library goals and figure out what macros we need to make them happen. Our goal is to produce the following API. Save this file as i18n.exs.

```
advanced_code_gen/i18n.exs
defmodule I18n do
  use Translator

  locale "en",
    flash: [
      hello: "Hello %{first} %{last}!",
      bye: "Bye, %{name}!"
    ],
    users: [
      title: "Users",
    ]

  locale "fr",
    flash: [
      hello: "Salut %{first} %{last}!",
      bye: "Au revoir, %{name}!"
    ],
    users: [
      title: "Utilisateurs",
    ]
end
```

Eventually we want to be able to call our module like this:

```
iex> I18n.t("en", "flash.hello", first: "Chris", last: "McCord")
"Hello Chris Mccord!"

iex> I18n.t("fr", "flash.hello", first: "Chris", last: "McCord")
"Salut Chris McCord!"

iex> I18n.t("en", "users.title")
"Users"
```

We'll support use Translator to allow any module to have a dictionary of translations compiled directly as t/3 function definitions. At minimum, we need to
define a _using_ macro to wire up some imports and attributes, and a locale
macro to handle locale registrations. Head back over to your editor, and let's
write some code.

Step 2: Implement a Skeleton Module with Metaprogramming Hooks

Our next step is to implement the skeleton of our Translator module by defining
the _using_, _before_compile_, and locale macros that we planned when fleshing
out the surface area of our API. The skeleton will simply set up the compile-
time hooks and module attribute registrations, but delegate the code generation bits to functions to be implemented later. Defining the metaprogramming
skeleton first will allow us to structure our module in a way that isolates the
advanced code generation to a function. This will keep our implementation
clear and reusable.

Create a translator.exs file with the following skeleton API:

```
advanced_code_gen/translator_step2.exs
Line 1  defmodule Translator do

        defmacro __using__(_options) do
          quote do
  5         Module.register_attribute __MODULE__, :locales, accumulate: true,
                                                            persist: false
            import unquote(__MODULE__), only: [locale: 2]
            @before_compile unquote(__MODULE__)
          end
 10     end

        defmacro __before_compile__(env) do
          compile(Module.get_attribute(env.module, :locales))
        end
 15
        defmacro locale(name, mappings) do
          quote bind_quoted: [name: name, mappings: mappings] do
            @locales {name, mappings}
          end
 20     end

        def compile(translations) do
          # TBD: Return AST for all translation function definitions
        end
 25   end
```

Just like our accumulated @tests attribute in our Assertion module from the
code on page 37, we registered an accumulated @locales attribute on line 5.

Next, we wired up the _before_compile_ hook in our Translator._using_ macro. On line 13, we added a placeholder to delegate to a compile function to carry out the code generation from our locale registrations, but we left the compile implementation for a later step. Finally, we defined our locale macro that will register a locale name and list of translations to be used by compile in our _before_compile_ hook.

With the accumulated attribute registrations wired up, we have all the necessary information to produce an AST of t/3 function definitions. If you like recursion, you're in for a treat. If not, pay attention and we'll break it down.

Step 3: Generate Code from Your Accumulated Module Attributes

Let's begin the bulk of our implementation by transforming the locale registrations into function definitions within our compile placeholder from Step 2. Our goal is to map our translations into a large AST of t/3 functions. We also need to add catch-all clauses that return {:error, :no_translation}. This will handle cases where no translation has been defined for the provided arguments.

Update your compile/1 function with the following code:

```
advanced_code_gen/translator_step3.exs
def compile(translations) do
  translations_ast = for {locale, mappings} <- translations do
    deftranslations(locale, "", mappings)
  end

  quote do
    def t(locale, path, bindings \\ [])
    unquote(translations_ast)
    def t(_locale, _path, _bindings), do: {:error, :no_translation}
  end
end

defp deftranslations(locales, current_path, mappings) do
  # TBD: Return an AST of the t/3 function defs for the given locale
end
```

On line 1, we defined our compile function to carry out the locale code generation. We used a for comprehension to map the locales into an AST of function definitions and stored the result in translations_ast for later injection. Next, we stubbed a deftranslations call that we'll implement later to define the t/3 functions. Finally, we produced an AST for the caller on lines 6–10 by combining our translations_ast with our catch-all functions.

Before we implement deftranslations, load your implementation in iex and let's check our progress:

```
iex> c "translator.exs"
[Translator]

iex> c "i18n.exs"
[I18n]

iex> I18n.t("en", "flash.hello", first: "Chris", last: "McCord")
{:error, :no_translation}

iex> I18n.t("en", "flash.hello")
{:error, :no_translation}
```

We're on the right track. Any call to I18n.t returns {:error, :no_translation} because we haven't yet generated the functions for each locale. We've confirmed that our catch-all t/3 definitions on line 9 were properly generated. Let's continue by implementing deftranslations to recursively walk our locales and define translation functions.

Fill in your deftranslations function with this code:

```
advanced_code_gen/translator_step4.exs
Line 1  defp deftranslations(locale, current_path, mappings) do
   -      for {key, val} <- mappings do
   -        path = append_path(current_path, key)
   -        if Keyword.keyword?(val) do
   5          deftranslations(locale, path, val)
   -        else
   -          quote do
   -            def t(unquote(locale), unquote(path), bindings) do
   -              unquote(interpolate(val))
   10           end
   -          end
   -        end
   -      end
   -    end
   15
   -    defp interpolate(string) do
   -      string # TBD interpolate bindings within string
   -    end
   -
   20   defp append_path("", next), do: to_string(next)
   -    defp append_path(current, next), do: "#{current}.#{next}"
```

We started by mapping over our translation key value pairs. Within our comprehension on line 4, we first checked whether the value is a keyword list. This would indicate a nested list of translation mappings, just like we saw in our original high-level API.

```
flash: [
  hello: "Hello %{first} %{last}!",
  bye: "Bye, %{name}!"
],
```

The :flash key above points to a nested keyword list of translations. To handle this, we would append "flash" to our accumulated current_path variable, which we handled by an append_path helper function on lines 20–21. Then we continue by recursively calling deftranslations until we encounter a string translation. We used quote on line 7 to generate the t/3 function definitions for each string and unquote to inject the proper current_path, such as "flash.hello", into the function clause. Our t/3 body called a stubbed interpolate function that we'll implement in a moment to take care of placeholder interpolations.

This required only a handful of lines of code, but the recursion can be a little mind-bending. Let's take a break and see where we're at in iex.

```
iex> c "translator.exs"
[Translator]

iex> c "i18n.exs"
[I18n]

iex> I18n.t("en", "flash.hello", first: "Chris", last: "McCord")
"Hello %{first} %{last}!"
```

We're nearly there. Our t/3 functions were correctly generated, and we just need to handle variable interpolation to complete our library. You might be wondering how we can keep track of all this code that we just generated. Like always, Elixir has us covered. When you start generating large amounts of code, it's often necessary to see the final source that is being produced. For this, you use Macro.to_string.

Macro.to_string: Make Sense of Your Generated Code

Macro.to_string takes an AST and produces a string of the high-level Elixir source. It's incredibly helpful when debugging your generated ASTs, especially for cases where many function heads are generated, such as in our Translator module. Let's inspect the generated code that compile has produced so far.

Add the following changes to your Translator module:

```
advanced_code_gen/macro_to_string.exs
Line 1  def compile(translations) do
   -      translations_ast = for {locale, mappings} <- translations do
   -        deftranslations(locale, "", mappings)
   -      end
   5
```

```
      final_ast = quote do
        def t(locale, path, binding \\ [])
        unquote(translations_ast)
        def t(_locale, _path, _bindings), do: {:error, :no_translation}
10    end

      IO.puts Macro.to_string(final_ast)
      final_ast
    end
```

On line 6, we stored the result of the generated AST in a final_ast binding. Then on line 12, we printed the entire AST expanded as Elixir source using Macro.to_string. To finish, we returned the final_ast as the last result to maintain the compile return signature. Load your file back up in iex, and let's see the results of our code generation so far:

```
iex> c "translator.exs"
[Translator]

iex> c "i18n.exs"
(
  def(t(locale, path, bindings \\ []))
  [[[def(t("fr", "flash.hello", bindings)) do
    "Salut %{first} %{last}!"
  end, def(t("fr", "flash.bye", bindings)) do
    "Au revoir, %{name}!"
  end], [def(t("fr", "users.title", bindings)) do
    "Utilisateurs"
  end]], [[def(t("en", "flash.hello", bindings)) do
    "Hello %{first} %{last}!"
  end, def(t("en", "flash.bye", bindings)) do
    "Bye, %{name}!"
  end], [def(t("en", "users.title", bindings)) do
    "Users"
  end]]]
  def(t(_locale, _path, _bindings)) do
    {:error, :no_translation}
  end
)
[I18n]
iex>
```

The results might look a little unusual at first, since our t/3 definitions are wrapped in a nested list. We see our def clauses within a list because our for comprehension returns a list of deftranslations ASTs. We could flatten and splice the list into the final AST, but Elixir doesn't mind definitions within lists, so we'll keep things simple by unquoting the list of definitions.

It's a good idea to use Macro.to_string any time you're generating an AST with many function definitions. You can see the final expanded code that will be injected into the caller and ensure that your generated arguments will be properly pattern matched. Of course, thorough testing is also helpful and shouldn't be skipped.

Final Step: Identify Areas for Compile-Time Optimizations

The final step of our Translator module is to interpolate values within the translation placeholders, such as Bye, %{name}!. While we could generate a regular expression to be evaluated at runtime, let's apply a compile-time optimization. We can generate a function definition that needs to perform string concatenation only when interpolating values. This will provide a huge performance boost at runtime. Let's complete our implementation by defining interpolate, whose job is to return the AST for our t/3 function bodies with interpolation where necessary.

```
advanced_code_gen/translator_final.exs
defp deftranslations(locale, current_path, mappings) do
  for {key, val} <- mappings do
    path = append_path(current_path, key)
    if Keyword.keyword?(val) do
      deftranslations(locale, path, val)
    else
      quote do
        def t(unquote(locale), unquote(path), bindings) do
          unquote(interpolate(val))
        end
      end
    end
  end
end

defp interpolate(string) do
  ~r/(?<head>)%{[^}]+}(?<tail>)/
  |> Regex.split(string, on: [:head, :tail])
  |> Enum.reduce "", fn
    <<"%{" <> rest>>, acc ->
      key = String.to_atom(String.rstrip(rest, ?}))
      quote do
        unquote(acc) <> to_string(Dict.fetch!(bindings, unquote(key)))
      end
    segment, acc -> quote do: (unquote(acc) <> unquote(segment))
  end
end
```

Starting on line 16, we split the translation string by the %{varname} pattern. Next, we reduce over each string segment and match on any segment starting with %{, which denotes a translation variable. When interpolated variables occur, we transform the Regex.split into a simple string concatenation AST. We use Dict.fetch! on the provided bindings variable to ensure the caller supplied all interpolated values. For regular string segments, we simply concatenate the accumulated AST. Let's check our solution using the Macro.to_string trick we saw earlier:

```
iex> c "translator.exs"
[Translator]

iex> c "i18n.exs"
(
  def(t(locale, path, binding \\ []))
  [[[def(t("fr", "flash.hello", bindings)) do
    (((("" <> "Salut ") <> to_string(Dict.fetch!(bindings, :first))) <> " ") <>
                        to_string(Dict.fetch!(bindings, :last))) <> "!"
  end, def(t("fr", "flash.bye", bindings)) do
    (("" <> "Au revoir, ") <> to_string(Dict.fetch!(bindings, :name))) <> "!"
  end], [def(t("fr", "users.title", bindings)) do
    "" <> "Utilisateurs"
  end]], [[def(t("en", "flash.hello", bindings)) do
    (((("" <> "Hello ") <> to_string(Dict.fetch!(bindings, :first))) <> " ") <>
                        to_string(Dict.fetch!(bindings, :last))) <> "!"
  end, def(t("en", "flash.bye", bindings)) do
    (("" <> "Bye, ") <> to_string(Dict.fetch!(bindings, :name))) <> "!"
  end], [def(t("en", "users.title", bindings)) do
    "" <> "Users"
  end]]]
  def(t(_locale, _path, _bindings)) do
    {:error, :no_translation}
  end
)
[I18n]

iex> I18n.t("en", "flash.hello", first: "Chris", last: "McCord")
"Hello Chris Mccord!"

iex> I18n.t("fr", "flash.hello", first: "Chris", last: "McCord")
"Salut Chris McCord!"

iex> I18n.t("en", "users.title")
"Users"
```

The ever-helpful Macro.to_string reveals the compile-time optimized function bodies for each t/3 definition. We can see that our interpolated ASTs properly expanded to simple string concatenation operations. This kind of performance optimization isn't possible in most languages and provides a substantial performance increase over relying on regular expressions at runtime.

You may be wondering how we were able to directly reference the bindings variable within interpolate without using the var! macro. We didn't have to worry about hygiene here because the quote blocks are all in the same module, so they share the same context. With the tricky parts out of the way, let's admire our work.

The Complete Translator Module

Let's take a look our completed library to see how all the pieces fit together. While you're reviewing the code, think about how each step of our metaprogramming rubric drove the design decisions of our final implementation.

```
advanced_code_gen/translator.exs
defmodule Translator do

  defmacro __using__(_options) do
    quote do
      Module.register_attribute __MODULE__, :locales, accumulate: true,
                                                       persist: false
      import unquote(__MODULE__), only: [locale: 2]
      @before_compile unquote(__MODULE__)
    end
  end

  defmacro __before_compile__(env) do
    compile(Module.get_attribute(env.module, :locales))
  end

  defmacro locale(name, mappings) do
    quote bind_quoted: [name: name, mappings: mappings] do
      @locales {name, mappings}
    end
  end

  def compile(translations) do
    translations_ast = for {locale, source} <- translations do
      deftranslations(locale, "", source)
    end

    quote do
      def t(locale, path, binding \\ [])
      unquote(translations_ast)
      def t(_locale, _path, _bindings), do: {:error, :no_translation}
    end
  end

  defp deftranslations(locale, current_path, translations) do
    for {key, val} <- translations do
      path = append_path(current_path, key)
```

```elixir
      if Keyword.keyword?(val) do
        deftranslations(locale, path, val)
      else
        quote do
          def t(unquote(locale), unquote(path), bindings) do
            unquote(interpolate(val))
          end
        end
      end
    end
  end

  defp interpolate(string) do
    ~r/(?<head>)%{[^}]+}(?<tail>)/
    |> Regex.split(string, on: [:head, :tail])
    |> Enum.reduce "", fn
      <<"%{" <> rest>>, acc ->
        key = String.to_atom(String.rstrip(rest, ?}))
        quote do
          unquote(acc) <> to_string(Dict.fetch!(bindings, unquote(key)))
        end
      segment, acc -> quote do: (unquote(acc) <> unquote(segment))
    end
  end

  defp append_path("", next), do: to_string(next)
  defp append_path(current, next), do: "#{current}.#{next}"
end
```

In 65 lines of code, we produced a robust internationalization library with compile-time optimized performance. By generating function heads for each translation mapping, we again let the Virtual Machine take over for fast lookup. Additional translations can simply be added by updating the locales.

Code Generation from Remote APIs

You took your metaprogramming skills to the next level with our last exercise and created a couple of essential tools to add to your Elixir arsenal. Now let's take a break from serious work and explore just how extensible Elixir really is. We aren't limited to generating code just from flat text files or Elixir data structures. Let's create a Hub mix project to define a module's functions directly from GitHub's public API. We'll produce a module that contains embedded information about our public repositories with the ability to launch a web browser directly to the project from a function call.

Mix Project Setup

Let's create a new mix project to house our implementation and application dependencies. After a couple of setup tasks, we should be on our way:

```
$ mix new hub --bare
$ cd hub
```

Next, we need to add Poison and HTTPotion to our mix dependencies for JSON encoding and performing HTTP requests.

hub/mix.exs
```
defmodule Hub.Mixfile do
  use Mix.Project

  def project do
    [app: :hub,
     version: "0.0.1",
     elixir: "~> 1.0.0",
     deps: deps]
  end

  def application do
    [applications: [:logger]]
  end

  defp deps do
    [{:ibrowse, github: "cmullaparthi/ibrowse", tag: "v4.1.0"},
     {:poison, "~> 1.3.0"},
     {:httpotion, "~> 1.0.0"}]
  end
end
```

Let's fetch our dependencies, and we should be ready to go:

```
$ mix deps.get
```

Remote Code Generation

Now let's open up our main hub.ex module and generate some code from a remote API. We'll hit GitHub's public API to fetch all the repositories under our GitHub usernames, and we'll decode the JSON body into an Elixir map. Next, we'll define a function from each result whose function name is the name of the repository and whose function body is all the data about each of our GitHub projects. Finally, we'll define a go function that accepts the name of a repository and launches a web browser to the URL. Here's a high-level overview:

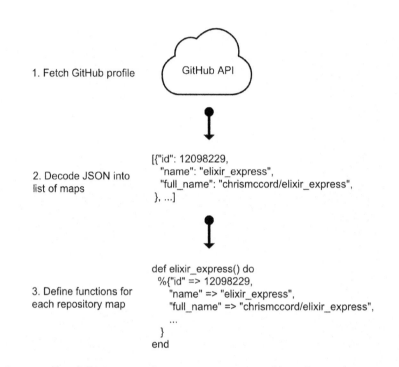

Now, key in the following code in your lib/hub.ex file. If you have a GitHub account, swap "chrismccord" with your own GitHub username.

```
hub/lib/hub.ex
Line 1  defmodule Hub do
          HTTPotion.start
          @username "chrismccord"

    5     "https://api.github.com/users/#{@username}/repos"
          |> HTTPotion.get(["User-Agent": "Elixir"])
          |> Map.get(:body)
          |> Poison.decode!
          |> Enum.each fn repo ->
   10       def unquote(String.to_atom(repo["name"]))() do
              unquote(Macro.escape(repo))
            end
          end

   15     def go(repo) do
            url = apply(__MODULE__, repo, [])["html_url"]
            IO.puts "Launching browser to #{url}..."
            System.cmd("open", [url])
          end
   20   end
```

On line 5, we began a pipeline to transform the JSON URL of our GitHub profile into a series of function definitions. We fetched the raw response body, decoded it as JSON, then mapped each JSON repository into function definitions. A function for each repository was defined by repo name; the function body simply contained the repo information. For convenience, we defined a go function on line 15 to quickly launch a browser window to a given repository's URL. Let's try it out in iex:

```
$ iex -S mix
```

```
iex> Hub.
atlas/0                        bclose.vim/0
calliope/0                     chrismccord.com/0
dot_vim/0                      elixir/0
elixir_express/0               ex_copter/0
genserver_stack_example/0      gitit/0
go/1                           haml-coffee/0
historian/0                    jazz/0
jellybeans.vim/0               labrador/0
linguist/0                     phoenix_chat_example/0
plug/0                         phoenix_haml/0
phoenix_render_example/0       phoenix_vs_rails_showdown/0

iex> Hub.linguist
%{"description" => "Elixir Internationalization library",
  "full_name" => "chrismccord/linguist",
  "git_url" => "git://github.com/chrismccord/linguist.git",
  "open_issues" => 4, "open_issues_count" => 4,
  "pushed_at" => "2014-08-04T13:28:30Z",
  "watchers" => 33,
  ...
}

iex> Hub.linguist["description"]
"Elixir Internationalization library"

iex> Hub.linguist["watchers"]
33

iex> Hub.go :linguist
Launching browser to https://github.com/chrismccord/linguist...
```

Let sink in for a moment what we just accomplished in 20 lines of code. We hit a remote JSON API over the Internet and embedded the data directly into a module as functions. The API call only happens a single time when the module is compiled. At runtime, we have the GitHub data cached directly within function definitions. While just a fun example, it really shows how Elixir lends itself to extension. Here we also saw Macro.escape for the first time.

Macro.escape

Macro.escape is used to take an Elixir literal and recursively escape it for injection into an AST. Its use is required when you need to inject an Elixir value into an already-quoted expression where the value is not an AST literal. For our Hub module, we need to inject the JSON map into the function body, but the def macro already quotes the received block of code. We escape repo when using unquote to convert the map into a valid AST for inclusion in the quoted block.

Open up iex, and let's try a couple of examples to see how it works:

```
iex> Macro.escape(123)
123

iex> Macro.escape([1, 2, 3])
[1, 2, 3]

iex> Macro.escape(%{watchers: 33, name: "linguist"})
{:%{}, [], [name: "linguist", watchers: 33]}

iex> defmodule MyModule do
...>    map = %{name: "Elixir"}
...>    def value do
...>       unquote(map)
...>    end
...> end
** (CompileError) iex: invalid quoted expression: %{name: "Elixir"}

iex> defmodule MyModule do
...>    map = Macro.escape %{name: "Elixir"}
...>    def value do
...>       unquote(map)
...>    end
...> end
{:module, MyModule, ...}

iex> MyModule.value
%{name: "Elixir"}
```

In our first MyModule example, we received a CompileError because the provided map was not a valid quoted expression. We fixed the expression by using Macro.escape to return an injectable AST. Any time you run into an *invalid quoted expression* error, take a step back and think about the quoted expressions you're trying to inject values into. If the expression is already quoted as an AST, Macro.escape will be required.

Further Exploration

We took our code generation experience to the next level by producing highly maintainable, performant programs that we can take and use in the services we build today. We saw the advantages of advanced code generation and had some fun generating code from remote APIs. If you're inspired by the possibilities of these techniques, try pushing further. Here are a few ideas to spark your imagination.

- Add a _using_ definition to the Mime module to allow arbitrary modules to use Mime and append their own custom MIME mappings, such as:

```
defmodule MimeMapper do
  use Mime, "text/emoji": [".emj"],
            "text/elixir": [".exs"]
end

iex> MimeMapper.exts_for_type("text/elixir")
[".exs"]

iex> MimeMapper.exts_for_type("text/html")
[".html"]
```

- Add pluralization support to your Translator module, such as:

```
iex> I18n.t("en", "title.users", count: 1)
"user"

iex> I18n.t("en", "title.users", count: 2)
"users"
```

- Generate code against your favorite web service with a public API.

CHAPTER 4

How to Test Macros

Any good library is only as reliable as the test suite behind it. You've written your own language features and a couple of essential application libraries. You even saw how macros let you create an expressive test framework. What you haven't seen yet is how to test macros themselves and the code generation they perform. We're going explore how to test macros so you can confidently maintain your libraries. You'll see few techniques for testing code generation and different test-case strategies for the types of metaprogramming involved.

Setting Up Your Test Suite

Running Elixir tests is usually just a matter of running mix test in your project's directory. If you need to test only a single file, Elixir makes it just as easy. Most of the exercises we've done so far have been single Elixir files, outside of a mix project. Let's see how easy it is to test them by setting up a test suite for the while macro we built in *Adding a while Loop to Elixir*, on page 22.

First things first: we need to create a test file. Launch your editor and create a while_test.exs file with the following code. Be sure to save it in the same directory as your while.exs file from the previous exercise.

```
macros/while_test_step1.exs
ExUnit.start
Code.require_file("while.exs", __DIR__)

defmodule WhileTest do
  use ExUnit.Case
  import Loop

  test "Is it really that easy?" do
    assert Code.ensure_loaded?(Loop)
  end
end
```

Now you can run your test suite with a simple call to elixir from the command line:

```
$ elixir while_test.exs
.

Finished in 0.04 seconds (0.04s on load, 0.00s on tests)
1 tests, 0 failures
```

That's all there is to it! Elixir's ExUnit test framework makes testing a first-class experience. This should leave you no excuse for not keeping your code well tested. With just a call to ExUnit.start and use ExUnit.Case, we were able to set up a test case for our Loop module, and we can see it's loaded and ready for some real assertions. Now that our test suite is set up, let's figure out what exactly needs to be tested in our Loop module.

Deciding What to Test

Your next step is deciding what needs to be tested. Entire books are written on this subject, and the answers vary. We'll review how to effectively test your while macro and ways to make assertions around stateful execution. It's important to avoid agonizing over what should be tested, how much, and whether you're abiding by a particular testing acronym. There's a handful of prominent testing methodologies and opinionated camps. Whether you're practicing test-driven development or red-green-refactor, or simply writing regression tests, the end result is the same. Choose a testing style that fits your mental workflow and keeps you happy. For some, that's TDD; for others, like me, it's prototype-driven development followed by regression tests and iteration. The important thing is that your library is tested. The methodology you choose is up to you. Try a few approaches and use what feels natural.

In most cases, you should test just enough to prove the correctness of your program. The goal shouldn't be to match lines upon lines of test code with library code. In fact, testing solely for code coverage ratios can lead to brittle tests.

To figure out how to test the accuracy of our while macro, let's list out its requirements:

- Execute a block of code repeatedly while a given expression is truthy.
- Use break to explicitly terminate execution.

That's it. Our test cases should go about proving these points. Let's write our first test case to verify that the while macro loops as long as its expression is truthy. Add the following code to your while_test.exs file:

```
macros/while_test.exs
```
```
Line 1  test "while/2 loops as long as the expression is truthy" do
   -      pid = spawn(fn -> :timer.sleep(:infinity) end)
   -
   -      send self, :one
   5      while Process.alive?(pid) do
   -        receive do
   -          :one -> send self, :two
   -          :two -> send self, :three
   -          :three ->
   10           Process.exit(pid, :kill)
   -            send self, :done
   -        end
   -      end
   -      assert_received :done
   15 end
```

We started the test case by exploiting processes and messages to mutate the result of our Process.alive?(pid) expression. On line 2, we spawned a process that sleeps forever so that it stays up and running. Next, we started a while loop on line 5, with our expression. To test that while loops as long as its expression is truthy, we sent ourselves a message before entering the loop to start a series of messages to handle within the loop.

Next, for each message we received, we sent another to ourselves to test the re-execution of the while block. After a couple loops of messages, we matched on the :three message and terminated our spawned pid. This will cause the next Process.alive?(pid) evaluation to return false and halt execution. We made sure to send ourselves a final message of :done that we later made an assertion about on line 14. If we receive the final message :done, we've proven that the while loop executed three times and then exited as expected.

Now let's run the tests:

```
$ elixir while_test.exs
.

Finished in 0.1 seconds (0.1s on load, 0.00s on tests)
1 tests, 0 failures
```

All green. We've proved the correctness of our first requirement. Now let's tackle the other half of our test suite by testing the break functionality. Update your file with this new test case:

```
macros/while_test.exs
```
```
Line 1  test "break/0 terminates execution" do
   -      send self, :one
   -      while true do
   -        receive do
```

```
5          :one -> send self, :two
           :two -> send self, :three
           :three ->
             send self, :done
             break
10      end
     end
     assert_received :done
  end
```

Our second test case is very similar to our first, but here we're testing that the break function halts execution of the loop. We start an infinite loop with while true, and much like before, we send and receive a series of messages to our own process to execute the loop a few times. On our third loop, we send ourselves a final message :done before calling break on line 9. We send this message so we can later assert the :done message was received, to ensure that the loop executed as we expected.

Again, let's see whether our tests pass:

```
$ elixir while_test.exs
..

Finished in 0.1 seconds (0.1s on load, 0.00s on tests)
2 tests, 0 failures
```

All tests pass again. That's all that is required to test our while macro. We used processes and messages to self for cheap and easy testing. Message-sending provided a way to assert that certain events happen in our loop, and the process trick allowed us to easily change the truthiness of the while expression on demand. Now that we've proven the correctness of our library, we can confidently iterate on new features and ensure that our macro still abides by the original requirements.

This macro was very simple to test because it performed only a small amount of code generation. More complex metaprogramming requires a different testing strategy.

Integration Testing

We did some advanced metaprogramming with our Mime and Translator libraries in Chapter 3, *Advanced Compile-Time Code Generation*, on page 43. Macro-driven libraries that generate large amounts of code are best tested at the integration level. Next, you'll find out what integration testing is all about and how we can apply it to the libraries we've written.

Test Your Generated Code, Not Your Code Generation

Integration testing means we test our library behavior at the top level. Given an input, we expect an output. We aren't so much concerned with testing the individual subcomponents. Testing macro-generated code in this way is effective because it's very difficult to isolate the AST transformation steps along the way. Instead, we use macros to generate code; then we test the expected behavior of the code, not the code-generation process itself.

Let's get a feel for this style of testing by writing a test suite for our Translator library we wrote in *Building an Internationalization Library*, on page 49. If you recall from our prior exercise, we used metaprogramming to inject many function clauses on a caller's I18n module. We recursed over a keyword list of translations and defined functions along the way.

To properly test this library, let's again break down the requirements. The Translator module has a handful of corner cases, so we'll outline them here as well.

- Generate t/3 functions while recursively walking all translations
- Allow multiple locales to be registered
- Handle nested translations
- Handle translations at the root level of the tree
- Support binding interpolation
- Raise an error unless all bindings have been provided for interpolation
- Return {:error, :no_translation} when no translation exists for the given input
- Convert any interpolation binding to string for proper concatenation

Not too bad, right? With our expected behavior outlined, let's go about integration-testing all the work Translator performs at compile time.

Easy Integration Testing with Nested Modules

We know what needs to be tested, but how do we go about testing Translator, since a caller's module is required to use Translator? Like most things in Elixir, it's easy. We can embed a module directly in our test module that uses Translator. When Elixir loads the test, our nested module will be compiled with all of the generated function definitions, and then we can make integration-level assertions around its behavior. Let's get to work.

Create a translator_test.exs file and add this initial code to it:

```
advanced_code_gen/translator_test_step1.exs
ExUnit.start
Code.require_file("translator.exs", __DIR__)

defmodule TranslatorTest do
  use ExUnit.Case

  defmodule I18n do
    use Translator

    locale "en", [
      foo: "bar",
      flash: [
        notice: [
          alert: "Alert!",
          hello: "hello %{first} %{last}!",
        ]
      ],
      users: [
        title: "Users",
        profile: [
          title: "Profiles",
        ]
    ]]

    locale "fr", [
      flash: [
        notice: [
          hello: "salut %{first} %{last}!"
        ]
    ]]
  end

  test "it recursively walks translations tree" do
    assert I18n.t("en", "users.title") == "Users"
    assert I18n.t("en", "users.profile.title") == "Profiles"
  end

  test "it handles translations at root level" do
    assert I18n.t("en", "foo") == "bar"
  end
end
```

Like our previous while_test.exs file, we made sure to start ExUnit and use ExUnit.Case to drive our test suite. Next, we defined a TranslatorTest module to house our tests. Then we defined a nested I18n module that calls use Translator. We registered an "en" and "fr" locale and added some filler translations that we can test against. The I18n module can then serve as the basis for the assertions of the test suite.

We built our assertions around the expected behavior of the functions that use Translator generated. We added the first two test cases and made assertions around the handling of nested and root-level translations.

Let's see how we're doing so far:

```
$ elixir translator_test.exs
..

Finished in 0.1 seconds (0.1s on load, 0.00s on tests)
2 tests, 0 failures
```

So far, so good. With a little prep work of creating a nested I18n module to integration-test against, we can continue testing the remaining requirements of our library.

Head back over to your editor, and let's complete the integration tests:

```
advanced_code_gen/translator_test.exs
test "it allows multiple locales to be registered" do
  assert I18n.t("fr", "flash.notice.hello", first: "Jaclyn", last: "M") ==
    "salut Jaclyn M!"
end

test "it iterpolates bindings" do
  assert I18n.t("en", "flash.notice.hello", first: "Jason", last: "S") ==
    "hello Jason S!"
end

test "t/3 raises KeyError when bindings not provided" do
  assert_raise KeyError, fn -> I18n.t("en", "flash.notice.hello") end
end

test "t/3 returns {:error, :no_translation} when translation is missing" do
  assert I18n.t("en", "flash.not_exists") == {:error, :no_translation}
end

test "converts interpolation values to string" do
  assert I18n.t("fr", "flash.notice.hello", first: 123, last: 456) ==
    "salut 123 456!"
end
```

We added test cases for the remaining items on our requirements list. We checked multiple locale registration, binding interpolation, error handling, and a couple of corner cases. The test cases were simple and succinct, which should be your goal. Your test descriptions should accurately describe what you're testing. If you find yourself writing really long test blocks, don't hesitate to split the assertions out into more refined test descriptions.

All that's left is to run our new tests:

```
$ elixir translator_test.exs
........

Finished in 0.1 seconds (0.1s on load, 0.00s on tests)
7 tests, 0 failures
```

All green. We have full integration coverage of our Translator library. Most of the time this is a perfect place to stop. Occasionally, though, complex macros should be tested at the unit level. Let's see how by adding unit tests to our Translator suite.

Unit Tests

Unit-testing macros should be used only for cases where you need to test a bit of tricky code generation in isolation. Over-testing macros at the unit level can lead to brittle tests because we can only test the AST generated from the macro or the string of source produced. These values can be hard to match against and are subject to change, which can lead to error-prone tests that are difficult to maintain.

Let's add unit tests to our Translator suite by testing the compile function. Our compile function was the main code-generation entry point that we delegated to from our __using__ macro. The easiest way to test that the t/3 functions were generated properly is to convert the AST to a string and test that the Elixir source matches what we expect.

Open up your translator_test.exs file and add these unit tests:

advanced_code_gen/translator_test.exs
```
test "compile/1 generates catch-all t/3 functions" do
  assert Translator.compile([]) |> Macro.to_string == String.strip ~S"""
  (
    def(t(locale, path, binding \\ []))
    []
    def(t(_locale, _path, _bindings)) do
      {:error, :no_translation}
    end
  )
  """
end

test "compile/1 generates t/3 functions from each locale" do
  locales = [{"en", [foo: "bar", bar: "%{baz}"]}]
  assert Translator.compile(locales) |> Macro.to_string == String.strip ~S"""
  (
    def(t(locale, path, binding \\ []))
    [[def(t("en", "foo", bindings)) do
      "" <> "bar"
```

```
    end, def(t("en", "bar", bindings)) do
      ("" <> to_string(Dict.fetch!(bindings, :baz))) <> ""
    end]]
    def(t(_locale, _path, _bindings)) do
      {:error, :no_translation}
    end
  )
  """
end
```

We tested the compile/1 function by using the Macro.to_string trick we learned when writing the Translator library. By piping the AST output of Translator.compile to Macro.to_string, we convert the AST into a string of Elixir source. This is easier to match against a large tuple of AST values. The only unit test cases we need are testing that the catch-all clauses are generated, followed by testing how nested translations are generated for each locale.

Let's run the tests:

```
$ elixir translator_test.exs
........

Finished in 0.1 seconds (0.1s on load, 0.00s on tests)
9 tests, 0 failures
```

Everything passes. As you can see, testing your macros directly against the string of code they produce isn't simple or pretty. It should be used only for isolated, complex cases like our recursive compile function. The vast majority of your code generation should be tested at the integration level.

With proper tests, our Translator library is now ready for production. We can be confident that our code generation is correct, and we can easily test for regressions as we extend the library with new features. This is what testing is all about. Not only does it prove the correctness of our code; it allows us to confidently make changes in the future. This is especially important for metaprogramming, where we must balance complexity and convenience.

Next, we'll review some testing tips to get the most out of your test suite.

Test Simple and Test Fast

If you've had experience with testing on large projects, there's a good chance you've experienced a frustratingly slow test suite. If running your tests is a slow and painful process, you're likely to stop writing tests altogether. Worse than slow tests are overly complex tests that take more work to change than the code itself. Let's see how you can avoid these pitfalls by following a couple of common conventions.

Limit the Number of Created Modules

When you integration-test your _using_ macros, like we did in our Translator tests, you have to create a module in the test to make assertions against. This is a perfect solution, but be aware that too many modules can cause unnecessarily slow load times when running your tests. You will often need to define multiple nested modules, but try to keep the number of modules you define to a minimum. Most times, multiple test cases can share the same module. Fast tests mean faster feedback cycles and a happy developer experience. Your goal should be to remove all possible friction between your code and your test suite.

Keep It Simple

The same rules that apply to metaprogramming and programming in general apply when writing tests. Keep it simple. If you have ever had the displeasure of working with a complex, brittle test suite on a large project, you know that you might spend more time getting the test suite to work than bringing your code up to new requirements. By keeping tests simple, you can allow the test cases to serve as specifications for the program. Properly written tests are often the first thing I look at when exploring how a new library works. Keeping them simple helps maintainability and provides a clear specification of your programs.

Further Exploration

You can now keep your macros well tested and well specified. Your testing skills will help you balance the complexity macros introduce with the payoff they provide in productivity and power. Apply the skills you've seen here, and don't worry too much about the testing methodologies you should use. Well-tested code is the goal; just make sure you make it happen.

Next, we'll create a full-featured domain-specific language. But first, try expanding your testing skills and have a little fun. Here are a couple of ideas to get you started.

- Let's get meta. Use your Assertion.assert macro to test your Translator and Loop macros. Instead of ExUnit, rewrite all the tests in this chapter to use our mini Assertion test framework. Our Assertion module didn't support assert_receive, so you'll have to get creative. Hint: Process.info(pid)[:messages] returns a list of messages in a process' mailbox.
- Add a test suite for our Mime library.

CHAPTER 5

Creating an HTML
Domain-Specific Language

One of the most powerful ways to use macros is to build domain-specific languages (DSLs). They let you create a custom layer in the language to attack problems closer to your application domain. This can make your code easier to write and make it more clearly represent the problem being solved. With DSLs, you can codify your business requirements and operate at a shared level of abstraction with the callers of your library.

Let's extend the tools you've learned so far to create an HTML DSL. We'll start by seeing what domain-specific languages are all about. Next, we'll build a complete HTML DSL that generates templates from pure Elixir code. While building our library, we'll uncover a few advanced macro features and see how to apply them. We'll finish by reviewing when and when not to use DSLs and ways to decide if they are a good fit for your library.

Getting Domain Specific

Before jumping into code, let's look at what DSLs are all about and how metaprogramming makes them so easy. In Elixir, DSLs are languages defined by custom macros. They are a way to build a language within a language for solving a specific domain problem. In our case, our domain is HTML generation.

You've probably had experience with HTML generation in other languages where the string of HTML was produced by mixing source code within markup, parsing the file, and evaluating the result. These solutions work, but you often have to leave pure source code behind for a different template syntax.

This requires yet another syntax to learn and context-switching between languages as your write your program.

Imagine if instead of parsing an external file, you could write regular Elixir code that expresses the HTML specification. The result of running the code would produce a complete HTML string. Let's see what such an HTML DSL might look like with macros:

```
markup do
  div class: "row" do
    h1 do
      text title
    end
    article do
      p do: text "Welcome!"
    end
  end
  if logged_in? do
    a href: "edit.html" do
      text "Edit"
    end
  end
end
"<div class\"row\"><h1>Domain Specific Languages</h1><article><p>Welcome!</p>
</article><a href=\"edit.html\">Edit</a></div>"
```

Since macros are first class features, we can imagine a macro per HTML tag that generates the necessary HTML string for a tree of tags. This example program is a complete domain-specific language. Any person who glances at the code would immediately understand the HTML specification being expressed by the source. Such a library would allow writing HTML and Elixir in the same context, leading to interesting solutions. This is the library that we'll be building. Let's get started.

Start by Defining the Minimum Viable API

Now that we know the kind of DSL that we would like to build, we need to decide how to design our API. The HTML spec includes some 117 valid tags, but we need a smaller surface area to begin our DSL. At this point you might be tempted to fire up your editor and start defining all 117 tags as individual macros. There's a better way. Since we define a mini language with macros when creating DSLs, the best way to begin is to define the smallest set of macros possible to serve as a basis for the broader macro DSL. Instead of immediately planning to support the entire HTML spec as macros, let's start with a refined set of macros that can still speak the HTML language.

The smallest API of our HTML library would contain a tag macro for tag construction, a text macro for injecting plain text, and a markup macro to wrap the entire generation block. These three macros will serve as a small, focused base of our implementation. They'll let us quickly get together a working version that we can enhance as we go.

Let's rewrite our previous example as if these were the only available macros:

```
markup do
  tag :div, class: "row" do
    tag :h1 do
      text title
    end
    tag :article do
      tag :p, do: text "Welcome!"
    end
  end
  if logged_in? do
    tag :a, href: "edit.html" do
      text "Edit"
    end
  end
end
"<div class\"row\"><h1>Domain Specific Languages</h1><article><p>Welcome!</p>
</article><a href=\"edit.html\">Edit</a></div>"
```

Supporting this reduced API will be the first step in building our HTML library. The reduced API isn't quite as nice as a full DSL, but we can still express the intent of our HTML generation. Once the initial macros are in place, we can go about supporting all 117 HTML tags using tag as the basis of each macro. Now that we know where to start, let's get to work.

Let's list the requirements of our minimum HTML API. First, it needs to support markup, tag, and text macros. The second and less obvious requirement is that our library must maintain an output buffer state while the markup is being generated. Because we can mix arbitrarily Elixir expressions within our DSL, we must store the state of the generated HTML as the program runs.

To understand why our library requires mutable state, let's imagine we tried to keep state by rebinding a buffer variable every time the tag macro was called. The comments below simulate the code we could generate to keep track of the buffer state in a buff variable as the program runs:

```
markup do          # buff = ""
  div do           # buff = buff <> "<div>"
    h1 do          # buff = buff <> "<h1>"
      text "hello" # buff = buff <> "hello"
    end            # buff = buff <> "</h1>"
```

```
    end            # buff = buff <> "</div>"
end                # buff

iex> buff
"<div><h1>hello</h1></div>"
```

By rebinding buff each time tag or text is called, this approach would work for basic cases. Before we rejoice about such a simple solution, consider what would happen if we added a for comprehension while using this approach:

```
markup do             # buff = ""
  tag :table do       # buff = buff <> "<table>
    tag :tr do         # buff = buff <> "<tr>"

      for i <- 0..3 do # >------->------->----------->
        tag :td do     # |  buff = buff <> "<td>"    |
          text "#{i}"  # ^  buff = buff <> "#{i}"    v
        end            # |  buff = buff <> "</td>"   |
      end              # <-------<-------<-----------<

    end                # buff = buff <> "</tr>"
  end                  # buff = buff <> "</table>"
end                    # buff

iex> buff
"<table><tr></tr></table>"
```

Everything looks good until we hit the for comprehension. Without a buffer process carrying the generated state, all of the td tags would be missing from the output because variable scoping prevents the nested bindings from leaking to the outside context. Even if we could get around scoping rules, the way rebinding works in Elixir would not support dynamically rebinding a variable this way within a for comprehension. You can see this for yourself by trying to rebind a variable in iex within a for block:

```
iex> buff = ""
""

iex> for i <- 1..3 do
...>   buff = buff <> "#{i}"
...>   IO.inspect buff
...> end
"1"
"2"
"3"
["1", "2", "3"]

iex> buff
""
```

As you can see, we cannot rely on variable rebinding to handle the output buffer. We must come up with a way to update the current buffer state each time tag or text is called. Fortunately, Elixir's Agent module provides a perfect way for us to keep track of the output buffer as each tag is generated.

Keeping State with Agents

Elixir Agents provide a simple way to store and retrieve state in your application. Let's see how easy it is to manage state with an Agent process. Go ahead and follow along in your own iex shell:

```
iex> {:ok, buffer} = Agent.start_link fn -> [] end
{:ok, #PID<0.130.0>}

iex> Agent.get(buffer, fn state -> state end)
[]

iex> Agent.update(buffer, &["<h1>Hello</h1>" | &1])
:ok

iex> Agent.get(buffer, &(&1))
["<h1>Hello</h1>"]

iex> for i <- 1..3, do: Agent.update(buffer, &["<td><#{i}</td>" | &1])
[:ok, :ok, :ok]

iex> Agent.get(buffer, &(&1))
["<td><3</td>", "<td><2</td>", "<td><1</td>", "<h1>Hello</h1>"]
```

The Agent module has a very small API that focuses on quick access to state. In the above example, we started an Agent with an initial state of []. Next, we prepended a few strings to its buffer list and closed by retrieving the updated state. We'll use a similar setup to store the output buffer of our HTML DSL.

Now that we refreshed our Agent skills, head back over to your editor and define an Html module within an html_step1.exs file and key in our minimal API:

```
html/lib/html_step1.exs
Line 1  defmodule Html do

        defmacro markup(do: block) do
          quote do
    5       {:ok, var!(buffer, Html)} = start_buffer([])
            unquote(block)
            result = render(var!(buffer, Html))
            :ok = stop_buffer(var!(buffer, Html))
            result
   10     end
        end
```

```
     def start_buffer(state), do: Agent.start_link(fn -> state end)

15   def stop_buffer(buff), do: Agent.stop(buff)

     def put_buffer(buff, content), do: Agent.update(buff, &[content | &1])

     def render(buff), do: Agent.get(buff, &(&1)) |> Enum.reverse |> Enum.join("")
20
     defmacro tag(name, do: inner) do
       quote do
         put_buffer var!(buffer, Html), "<#{unquote(name)}>"
         unquote(inner)
25       put_buffer var!(buffer, Html), "</#{unquote(name)}>"
       end
     end

     defmacro text(string) do
30     quote do: put_buffer(var!(buffer, Html), to_string(unquote(string)))
     end
   end
```

On line 3, we defined the markup macro, which wraps the entire HTML generation block. Within markup, we perform three actions. First, we start an Agent
with start_buffer that we defined on line 13. The Agent will hold a list of all tag
or text outputs. Next, we injected the block of code passed from the caller,
which contains all their tag and text macro calls. We finished the markup block
by calling render, which we defined on line 19. The render function gets the
Agent's state and combines all buffer segments to form the final output string.
Next, we make sure to stop the Agent process before returning the result now
that its work is complete.

Apart from our markup block and Agent functions, we also defined the tag and
text macros on lines 21 and 29 to complete our essential macro set. The tag
definition wraps the caller's inner code block with put_buffer calls. This surrounds
the inner contents in an opening and closing HTML tag. For example, let's
see how this would work with a nested series of tags:

```
tag :div do
  tag: span do
    Logger.info "We can mix regular Elixir code here"
    text "Nested tags are no trouble for our buffer"
  end
end
```

At compile time, this block of code would turn into:

```
put_buffer(var!(buffer, Html), "<div>")
put_buffer(var!(buffer, Html), "<span>")
```

```
Logger.info "We can mix regular Elixir code here"
put_buffer(var!(buffer, Html), "Nested tags are no trouble for our buffer")
put_buffer(var!(buffer, Html), "</span>")
put_buffer(var!(buffer, Html), "</div>")
```

Not much to it, right? With the Agent keeping state, the tag macro just needs to generate the correct put_buffer calls and ensure that any nested block is wrapped with opening and closing tags. Similarly, the text macro only needs to generate a single put_buffer call while converting its argument to a string.

Overriding Hygiene Is a Necessary Evil. Use with Care.

One important note about our implementation is the fact that we are overriding hygiene when accessing the buffer variable throughout the module. Overriding hygiene allows us to reference the spawned Agent's process throughout each independent quote block because we explicitly use var! to reach outside the given context. Most importantly, we pass Html as the second argument so that the buffer variable's context stays in our module. If we did not include the Html argument, our buffer variable would leak into the caller's context and become accessible in their code. This is one example where overriding hygiene is a worthy tradeoff. We can implicitly store state behind the scenes from the caller and avoid clashes by generating the buffer variable in our Html context.

Try It Out

Let's define a quick Template module to see our minimally viable API in action. Add the following code to a new html_step1_render.exs file:

html/lib/html_step1_render.exs
```
Line 1  defmodule Template do
          import Html

          def render do
    5       markup do
              tag :table do
                tag :tr do
                  for i <- 0..5 do
                    tag :td, do: text("Cell #{i}")
    10            end
                end
              end
              tag :div do
                text "Some Nested Content"
    15        end
            end
          end
        end
```

On line 4, we defined an arbitrary render function to house our markup generation. Now, let's load it up in iex and try it out:

```
iex> c "html_step1.exs"
[Html]

iex> c "html_step1_render.exs"
[Template]

iex> Template.render
"<table><tr><td>Cell 0</td><td>Cell 1</td><td>Cell 2</td><td>Cell 3</td>
<td>Cell 4</td><td>Cell 5</td></tr></table><div>Some Nested Content</div>"
```

Using only the markup, tag, and text macros, we generated a string of HTML while transparently storing state behind the scenes in our buffer Agent. Our DSL is starting to speak its first few words. Next, we'll make it fluent by supporting the full HTML spec.

Support the Entire HTML Spec with Macros

We're off to a great start, but our goal is to create a first-class DSL. A single tag macro simply won't cut it. Let's up our sophistication by supporting all 117 valid HTML tags. We could write a hundred macros by hand, but let's use the techniques you learned in Chapter 3, *Advanced Compile-Time Code Generation*, on page 43, to save time and effort.

As before, a quick Internet search turned up a complete list of HTML tags.[1] After a copy and paste into a flat text file, we end with a file of line-delimited tags. Here's a handful of lines from the file:

```
html/lib/tags.txt
form
frame
frameset
h1
head
header
```

We'll use this file to generate the entire HTML spec. Copy the file over to your own project and save it as tags.txt within the same folder as your Html module. Now, head back over to your Html source file and let's parse tags.txt into macro definitions. We'll save the new file as html_step2.exs.

---

1.   http://www.html-5-tutorial.com/all-html-tags.htm

```
html/lib/html_step2.exs
Line 1  defmodule Html do

          @external_resource tags_path = Path.join([__DIR__, "tags.txt"])
          @tags (for line <- File.stream!(tags_path, [], :line) do
    5         line |> String.strip |> String.to_atom
          end)

          for tag <- @tags do
            defmacro unquote(tag)(do: inner) do
   10         tag = unquote(tag)
              quote do: tag(unquote(tag), do: unquote(inner))
            end
          end

   15     defmacro markup(do: block) do
            quote do
              import Kernel, except: [div: 2]
              {:ok, var!(buffer, Html)} = start_buffer([])
              unquote(block)
   20         result = render(var!(buffer, Html))
              :ok = stop_buffer(var!(buffer, Html))
              result
            end
          end
   25     # ...
```

On line 4, we mapped over our tags.txt file, line by line, and stored the tag names as a list of atoms on the @tags attribute. Next, we used another for comprehension on line 8 to define one macro for every tag whose name is the tag name converted to an atom. Each macro simply proxies to the tag definition that we defined in our first step.

Another important task was to exclude Kernel.div from being imported into our markup block on line 17 and clashing with the common <div> tag. Having Kernel.div unavailable is an okay tradeoff because it can still be explicitly invoked from the Kernel module as needed. We also used @external_resource again to ensure that our Html module is recompiled by mix any time the tags.txt file changes.

Let's render some HTML with our new macros. Create a new Template module with the following code and save it as html_step2_render.exs:

html/lib/html_step2_render.exs
```elixir
defmodule Template do
  import Html

  def render do
    markup do
      table do
        tr do
          for i <- 0..5 do
            td do: text("Cell #{i}")
          end
        end
      end
      div do
        text "Some Nested Content"
      end
    end
  end
end
```

We replaced all tag calls with the new macros that we just generated. Let's try it out in iex:

```elixir
iex> c "html_step2.exs"
[Html]

iex> c "html_step2_render.exs"
[Template]

iex> Template.render
"<table><tr><td>Cell 0</td><td>Cell 1</td><td>Cell 2</td><td>Cell 3</td><td>Cell 4</td><td>Cell 5</td></tr></table><div>Some Nested Content</div>"
```

It works! We took advantage of compile-time code generation to support the entire HTML specification as a DSL. Going from a DSL made of three macros to one made of more than a hundred required only a small amount of clean, maintainable code. As future HTML tags are introduced, we need to edit only the tags.txt file to support the latest specification.

We've come a long way with our DSL, but we're not finished yet. Let's continue by supporting other common HTML features.

Enhance Your API with HTML Attribute Support

If we want our HTML library to be truly useful to the world, we need to add support for tag attributes such as class and id. Let's extend our DSL to support an optional keyword list that gets translated into tag attributes for each macro. For example, our goal is to support the following API:

```
div id: "main" do
  h1 class: "title", do: text("Welcome!")
  div class: "row" do
    div class: "column" do
      p "Hello!"
    end
  end
  button onclick: "javascript: history.go(-1);" do
    text "Back"
  end
end
```

Let's revisit our Html module and add support for tag attributes. Replace your tag/2 macro and for tag <- @tags comprehension with the following code. Save the updated listing as html_step3.exs.

html/lib/html_step3.exs

```
Line 1  for tag <- @tags do
        defmacro unquote(tag)(attrs, do: inner) do
          tag = unquote(tag)
          quote do: tag(unquote(tag), unquote(attrs), do: unquote(inner))
     5  end
        defmacro unquote(tag)(attrs \\ []) do
          tag = unquote(tag)
          quote do: tag(unquote(tag), unquote(attrs))
        end
    10  end

        defmacro tag(name, attrs \\ []) do
          {inner, attrs} = Dict.pop(attrs, :do)
          quote do: tag(unquote(name), unquote(attrs), do: unquote(inner))
    15  end
        defmacro tag(name, attrs, do: inner) do
          quote do
            put_buffer var!(buffer, Html), open_tag(unquote_splicing([name, attrs]))
            unquote(inner)
    20      put_buffer var!(buffer, Html), "</#{unquote(name)}>"
          end
        end

        def open_tag(name, []), do: "<#{name}>"
    25  def open_tag(name, attrs) do
          attr_html = for {key, val} <- attrs, into: "", do: " #{key}=\"#{val}\""
          "<#{name}#{attr_html}>"
        end
```

On line 1 we modified our for comprehension to generate multiple macro heads for each tag. This allows an optional attrs list to be passed to the macros. Along the same lines, we added an extra tag macro to handle optional attributes. On line 24, we defined open_tag functions to handle building an HTML tag with a list of attributes. We then delegated to this function within our modified tag definition. Here we also used unquote_splicing for the first time.

The unquote_splicing macro behaves much like unquote, except it injects a list of arguments to an AST instead of a single value. For example, the following blocks of code are equivalent:

```
quote do
  put_buffer var!(buffer), open_tag(unquote_splicing([name, attrs]))
end
quote do
  put_buffer var!(buffer), open_tag(unquote(name), unquote(attrs))
end
```

unquote_splicing is convenient when you want to inject a list of arguments, especially if those arguments are of variable length at compile time.

With our new attribute support in place, let's head back to iex and see how it works. Update your Template module with the following code and save it as html_step3_render.exs. Feel free to generate your own HTML tags and attributes as you try it out.

```
html/lib/html_step3_render.exs
defmodule Template do
  import Html

  def render do
    markup do
      div id: "main" do
        h1 class: "title" do
          text "Welcome!"
        end
      end
      div class: "row" do
        div do
          p do: text "Hello!"
        end
      end
    end
  end
end
```

Now load both files into iex and render the template you just created.

```
iex> c "html_step3.exs"
[Html]

iex> c "html_step3_render.exs"
[Template]
```

```
iex> Template.render
"<div id=\"main\"><h1 class=\"title\">Welcome!</h1>
</div><div class=\"row\"><div><p>Hello!</p></div></div>"
```

Great work! We now have a robust HTML DSL that is easy to read and write. You can define entire templates for a web application with pure Elixir code and easily extend the library as the HTML specification grows to support new tags. At 60 lines of code, our DSL has a tiny footprint, even with support for more than a hundred macros.

But, we're not stopping there. Next, you'll find out ways Elixir lets us trim this footprint down even further.

Generate Less Code by Walking the AST

Our Html module is clear and concise, but we did have to generate well over a hundred macros to make it work. Wouldn't it be nice to generate less code but still maintain our expressive DSL where all tags can be used as macro calls? Let's make it happen.

You might think that maintaining our DSL without generating all HTML macros sounds impossible, but step back and remember that Elixir gives you full AST access. For example, open up an iex prompt and quote a few arbitrary HTML DSL expressions, and let's look at the results. Do not load your Html module since we are just quoting raw expressions outside the context of our library for this example.

```
iex> ast = quote do
...>    div do
...>      h1 do
...>        text "Hello"
...>      end
...>    end
...> end
{:div, [], [[do: {:h1, [], [[do: {:text, [], ["Hello"]}]]}]]}
```

Looks pretty simple, right? We received the AST representation of the macro DSL in the form we first saw in *The Structure of the AST*, on page 8. We can see our macro calls are neatly nested in a series of three-element tuples. Now imagine instead of generating all HTML tags as macros, we could instead walk the AST, piece by piece, and convert the AST nodes like {:div, [] [[do: ...]]} into tag :div do ... macro calls. In fact, Elixir comes built in with functions to help us do this.

Elixir contains the Macro.prewalk/2 and Macro.postwalk/2 functions that allow you to walk an AST depth-first or breadth-first. Let's use IO.inspect to see what happens if we walk the AST for our quoted expression that we bound to the ast variable above:

```
iex> Macro.postwalk ast, fn segment -> IO.inspect(segment) end
:do
:do
"Hello"
{:text, [], ["Hello"]}
{:do, {:text, [], ["Hello"]}}
[do: {:text, [], ["Hello"]}]
{:h1, [], [[do: {:text, [], ["Hello"]}]]}
{:do, {:h1, [], [[do: {:text, [], ["Hello"]}]]}}
[do: {:h1, [], [[do: {:text, [], ["Hello"]}]]}]
{:div, [], [[do: {:h1, [], [[do: {:text, [], ["Hello"]}]]}]]}
{:div, [], [[do: {:h1, [], [[do: {:text, [], ["Hello"]}]]}]]}

iex> Macro.prewalk ast, fn segment -> IO.inspect(segment) end
{:div, [], [[do: {:h1, [], [[do: {:text, [], ["Hello"]}]]}]]}
[do: {:h1, [], [[do: {:text, [], ["Hello"]}]]}]
{:do, {:h1, [], [[do: {:text, [], ["Hello"]}]]}}
:do
{:h1, [], [[do: {:text, [], ["Hello"]}]]}
[do: {:text, [], ["Hello"]}]
{:do, {:text, [], ["Hello"]}}
:do
{:text, [], ["Hello"]}
"Hello"
{:div, [], [[do: {:h1, [], [[do: {:text, [], ["Hello"]}]]}]]}
```

If we look closely, we can see that Macro.postwalk and Macro.prewalk walked the AST and passed each segment to our function. We can also clearly see our macro calls within segments like {:text, [], ["Hello"]}. These functions can be used to augment the AST, but we only printed the value and returned the result untouched.

Let's remove all 117 generated macros in our Html module. We'll replace them by generating code as we walk the AST. Update your Html module with the following listing and save it as html_macro_walk.exs:

```
html/lib/html_macro_walk.exs
Line 1  defmodule Html do

          @external_resource tags_path = Path.join([__DIR__, "tags.txt"])
          @tags (for line <- File.stream!(tags_path, [], :line) do
     5        line |> String.strip |> String.to_atom
          end)

          defmacro markup(do: block) do
            quote do
    10        {:ok, var!(buffer, Html)} = start_buffer([])
```

```
         unquote(Macro.postwalk(block, &postwalk/1))
         result = render(var!(buffer, Html))
         :ok = stop_buffer(var!(buffer, Html))
         result
15     end
     end

     def postwalk({:text, _meta, [string]}) do
       quote do: put_buffer(var!(buffer, Html), to_string(unquote(string)))
20     end
     def postwalk({tag_name, _meta, [[do: inner]]}) when tag_name in @tags do
       quote do: tag(unquote(tag_name), [], do: unquote(inner))
     end
     def postwalk({tag_name, _meta, [attrs, [do: inner]]}) when tag_name in @tags do
25     quote do: tag(unquote(tag_name), unquote(attrs), do: unquote(inner))
     end
     def postwalk(ast), do: ast

     def start_buffer(state), do: Agent.start_link(fn -> state end)
30
     def stop_buffer(buff), do: Agent.stop(buff)

     def put_buffer(buff, content), do: Agent.update(buff, &[content | &1])

35   def render(buff), do: Agent.get(buff, &(&1)) |> Enum.reverse |> Enum.join("")

     defmacro tag(name, attrs \\ [], do: inner) do
       quote do
         put_buffer var!(buffer, Html), open_tag(unquote_splicing([name, attrs]))
40       unquote(postwalk(inner))
         put_buffer var!(buffer, Html), unquote("</#{name}>")
       end
     end

45   def open_tag(name, []), do: "<#{name}>"
     def open_tag(name, attrs) do
       attr_html = for {key, val} <- attrs, into: "", do: " #{key}=\"#{val}\""
       "<#{name}#{attr_html}>"
     end
50 end
```

We started by updating our markup definition on line 11 to call Macro.postwalk against the block of code passed from the caller. On lines 18 through 27, we replaced our for comprehension, which generated all 117 tag macros, with just four postwalk functions. These four functions use basic pattern matching to pluck out AST segments and transform them into the correct HTML tag. Let's break down how these little functions are able to perform so much work.

The postwalk function on line 18 pattern matches on the AST segment of a text macro call and returns a quoted put_buffer call. The argument is converted to a string, just like the text macro definition in our previous step. Next, we pattern match on the AST segment of all 117 HTML tags on line 21. Here we use a guard of when tag_name in @tags to match on the first element of the AST tuple. If we find a segment matching an HTML tag, we convert it into a tag macro call. Lastly, on line 27, we add a catch-all postwalk function that returns any segment untouched that we don't identify as part of our DSL. Let's use the trick that we learned in *Macro.to_string: Make Sense of Your Generated Code*, on page 53, to see the code that our postwalk functions produce.

Head back to iex, load up your html_macro_walk.exs file, and follow along:

```
iex> c "html_macro_walk.exs"
[Html]

iex> import Html
nil

iex> ast = quote do
...>   markup do
...>     div do
...>       h1 do
...>         text "Some text"
...>       end
...>     end
...>   end
...> end

iex> ast |> Macro.expand(__ENV__) |> Macro.to_string |> IO.puts
(
  {:ok, var!(buffer, Html)} = start_buffer([])
  tag(:div, []) do
    tag(:h1, []) do
      put_buffer(var!(buffer, Html), to_string("Some text"))
    end
  end
  result = render(var!(buffer, Html))
  :ok = stop_buffer(var!(buffer, Html))
  result
)
:ok
```

We quoted an example markup block and used Macro.expand and Macro.to_string to peek at the code produced by our postwalk transformations. We can see that the postwalk functions properly transformed the HTML tags into tag macro calls.

This was an advanced exercise full of specialized pattern matching against the raw AST. Don't fret if it takes you a moment to understand how it works. Macro.postwalk walks the AST and lets you transform each segment, so you can see how we matched against the segments we cared about to do all the work of the 117 macros that we replaced. You won't need to reach for Macro.postwalk or Macro.prewalk often, but having them in the back of your metaprogramming arsenal is convenient for cases where you want to transform an entire AST without defining each and every macro contained within the quoted expression.

Now that you've leveled up on your domain-specific language experience, we need to review when and where DSLs are appropriate.

To DSL or Not to DSL?

So DSLs are pretty cool, huh? It's tempting to solve all kinds of problems this way, but be careful. Many problems that seem like a good fit for a DSL are often better served by standard functions. Whenever I'm trying to decide whether a DSL is a good fit, I ask myself the following questions:

1. Can the domain be expressed naturally by macros in Elixir's syntax, such as HTML tags?
2. Would a DSL cause the caller to think more or less about how to solve their problem?
3. Should I require users of my library to have all kinds of code injected into their context?

The answers to these questions vary, and many times it's a gray area. To help illustrate these points, let's imagine a fictitious Emailer library that we would like to build. At first glance, the email domain can be expressed very simply by words like from, to, subject, send. So it seems an email library would meet the requirements of #1, where the problem can be naturally expressed by macros. With that thought, let's imagine what our library could look like as a DSL:

```
defmodule UserWelcomeEmail do
  use Emailer

  from     "info@example.com"
  reply_to "info@example.com"
  subject  "Welcome!"

  def deliver(to, body) do
    send_email to: to, body: body
  end
end

UserWelcomeEmail.deliver("user@example.com", "Hello there!")
```

Not too bad, right? Callers could use Emailer and have a DSL defined for wiring up email headers, such as from, reply_to, etc. This reads nicely, but now ask yourself #2 above. Would this DSL cause the caller to think more or less about how to solve their problem? For example, what if the caller needs to add custom extension headers, such as "X-SERVICE-ID"? The email spec supports arbitrary headers, so this suddenly puts our DSL into a snag. One quick solution would be to support an optional headers function that the caller can implement to add custom headers:

```
defmodule UserWelcomeEmail do
  use Emailer

  from     "info@example.com"
  reply_to "info@example.com"
  subject  "Welcome!"

  def headers do
    %{"X-SERVICE-ID" => "myservice"}
  end

  def deliver(to, body) do
    send_email to: to, body: body
  end
end
```

This works, but now the caller must know or look up which headers are supported by the DSL and which times they need to define a headers map. Now let's consider an API without a DSL. It would simply require the caller to define a headers function that returns a map of all email headers they require.

```
defmodule UserWelcomeEmail do
  use Emailer

  def headers do
    %{"from"         => "info@example.com",
      "reply-to"     => "info@example.com",
      "subject"      => "Welcome!",
      "X-SERVICE-ID" => "myservice"}
  end

  def deliver(to, body) do
    send_email to: to, body: body
  end
end
```

In this case, the non-DSL approach wins out. The usage is clear and still reads nicely without the need for a DSL.

The last point to consider when weighing the options for a DSL is to think about whether a caller really needs a bunch of code injected into its module. Sometimes the clear answer is yes, but other times having all kinds of macros and code injected into your module, just for simple actions like sending an email, is less desirable. It can clash with user code and add complexity where functions would have otherwise been a more appropriate solution.

Based on this, the Emailer library would not make a good DSL. Explicit functions provide an easier-to-use API without the need to learn a special DSL just to send an email message. DSLs are a powerful tool, but you should think carefully about whether they accurately solve your domain problem. They allow a simplified API for problem solving, but sometimes this can become restrictive. Their use should be determined on a case-by-case basis, and it helps to ask yourself those three questions every time you think DSLs might be a good choice.

Further Exploration

You leveled up on your metaprogramming skills by defining a language within a language using DSLs. This style of problem solving will let you create expressive libraries that can distill a problem into a natural set of macros. You saw how some domains, like HTML generation, fall naturally into a DSL, while others require careful consideration of tradeoffs. Think about other ways you can extend the HTML DSL to make it production ready. Here are some ideas to get you started:

- Extend the Html library with nicely formatted output:

```
iex> Template.render
"<div id=\"main\">
  <h1 class=\"title\">Welcome!</h1>
</div>
<div class=\"row\">
  <div>
    <p>Hello!</p>
  </div>
</div>"
```

- Sanitize all text input against cross-site-scripting attacks:

```
defmodule Template do
  import Html

  def render do
    markup do
      div id: "main" do
```

```
        text "XSS Protection <script>alert('vulnerable?');</script>"
      end
    end
  end
end

iex> Template.render
"<div id=\"main\">
  XSS Protection &lt;script&gt;alert(&#39;vulnerable?&#39;);&lt;/script&gt;
</div>"
```

CHAPTER 6

With Great Power Comes Great Responsibility (and Fun!)

We've unlocked Elixir's metaprogramming secrets. We went from the basics all the way to writing our own languages features. Along the way, you gained insight into Elixir's internals, and if you're like me, you found a new found appreciation for the language's syntax and idioms. Without curbing your excitement, we're going to review some tips and tricks for getting the most out of Elixir's macro system and how you can avoid common pitfalls. Staying on the happy path of metaprogramming will let you write extensible code that is easy to write and maintain.

When and Where to Use Macros

Because Elixir is a language built on top of macros, it's easy to think that every library you write needs macros. This isn't the case. Macros should be reserved for specialized cases where the solution can't be implemented easily as normal function definitions. Whenever you're writing code and reach for defmacro, stop and ask yourself whether your solution requires code generation. Sometimes code generation is absolutely required, but other times it's easy to get carried away with macros where you could've just written functions instead.

In some cases, the choice for macros is easy. For things like control flow, where access to the AST expression is required, macros are the obvious choice. For example, let's imagine trying to implement if as a function instead of a macro, like our implementation in *Re-Creating the if Macro*, on page 22:

```
iex> defmodule ControlFlow do
...>   def if(expr, do: block, else: else_block) do
...>     case expr do
...>       result when result in [nil, false] -> else_block
...>       result -> block
...>     end
...>   end
...> end
{:module, ControlFlow,
<<70, 79, 82, 49, 0, 0, 5, 120, 66, 69, 65, 77, 69, 120, 68, ...

iex> ControlFlow.if true do
...>   IO.puts "It's true!"
...> else
...>   IO.puts "It's false!"
...> end
It's true!
It's false!
```

What happened? Both of the IO.puts expressions were evaluated because they were passed to the if function at runtime. Macros are an obvious requirement here because we must convert the expression at compile time into a case expression to avoid runtime evaluation of both clauses. Other times the choice is not as obvious.

In creating Phoenix,[1] an Elixir web framework, I used macros for its router layer. The case for macros in the Phoenix router is twofold. First, it allows for an expressive and easy-to-use routing DSL. Second, it can generate many clauses internally that a user would've had to write by hand. Let's look at a high-level overview of the kind of code the router generates. Then we can talk about the macro tradeoffs.

Here's a minimal Phoenix router that routes HTTP requests to controller modules:

```
defmodule MyRouter do
  use Phoenix.Router

  pipeline :browser do
    plug :accepts, ~w(html)
    plug :fetch_session
  end

  scope "/" do
    pipe_through :browser

    get "/pages", PageController, :index
```

---

1. http://www.phoenixframework.org

```
    get "/pages/:page", PageController, :show
    resources "/users", UserController do
      resources "/comments", CommentController
    end
  end
end
```

After MyRouter is compiled, Phoenix generates function heads on the module that look something like this:

```
defmodule MyRouter do
  ...
  def match(conn, "GET",    ["pages"])
  def match(conn, "GET",    ["pages", page])
  def match(conn, "GET",    ["users", "new"])
  def match(conn, "POST",   ["users"])
  def match(conn, "PUT",    ["users", id])
  def match(conn, "PATCH",  ["users", id])
  def match(conn, "DELETE", ["users", id])
  def match(conn, "GET",    ["users", user_id, "comments"])
  def match(conn, "GET",    ["users", user_id, "comments", id, "edit"])
  def match(conn, "GET",    ["users", user_id, "comments", id])
  def match(conn, "GET",    ["users", user_id, "comments", "new"])
  def match(conn, "POST",   ["users", user_id, "comments"])
  def match(conn, "PUT",    ["users", user_id, "comments", id])
  def match(conn, "PATCH",  ["users", user_id, "comments", id])
  def match(conn, "DELETE", ["users", user_id, "comments", id])
end
```

The Phoenix router uses macros such as get, post, and resources to convert an HTTP DSL into a series of match/3 definitions. I chose to use macros for Phoenix's router because after weighing the tradeoffs, I decided that the routing DSL not only provides a high-level API for routing HTTP requests, but it also removes dozens of lines of boilerplate that would need to be written by hand. This does come at a cost of code-generation complexity, but the payoffs make macros a clear win.

Macros require careful consideration on the balance of convenience over complexity. When using macros in Phoenix, I strive for the simplest solution possible. The caller trusts that the generated code is simple and fast. This should be your implicit contract with the caller for any code you generate.

The most important metaprogramming strategy is to keep it simple. Striking a balance between library power, ease of use, and internal complexity is a careful game you must play. Next, you'll see how to keep it simple and which hazards to avoid.

Avoiding Common Pitfalls

As with any powerful tool, it's easy to cut yourself. Throughout my Elixir experience, a few common mistakes have appeared that are easy to avoid in retrospect but can wreak havoc on your code base over time if ignored. Let's find out ways to avoid getting caught in your own web of code generation.

Don't use When You Can import

One of the most common mistakes newly minted metaprogrammers make is treating use as a way to mix in functions from other modules. This tempting idea conflates the concept of a mix-in from other languages, where you can include methods and functions from one module into another. In Elixir, this pitfall looks something like this.

Consider a StringTransforms module that defines a number of string transformation functions to use around your code base. You might write something like this for easy sharing across different modules:

```
Line 1  defmodule StringTransforms do
    -     defmacro __using__(_opts) do
    -       quote do
    -         def title_case(str) do
    5           str
    -           |> String.split(" ")
    -           |> Enum.map(fn <<first::utf8, rest::binary>> ->
    -             String.upcase(List.to_string([first])) <> rest
    -           end)
    10          |> Enum.join(" ")
    -         end
    -
    -         def dash_case(str) do
    -           str
    15          |> String.downcase
    -           |> String.replace(~r/[^\w]/, "-")
    -         end
    -         # ... hundreds of more lines of string transform functions
    -       end
    20    end
    -   end

    -   defmodule User do
    -     use StringTransforms
    25
    -     def friendly_id(user) do
    -       dash_case(user.name)
    -     end
    -   end
```

30

```
iex> User.friendly_id(%{name: "Elixir Lang"})
"elixir-lang"
```

On line 2, a __using__ macro is defined to house a quoted expression of some string transformation functions, such as title_case and dash_case. On line 24, the User module uses StringTransforms so that the functions are injected into its context. This allows dash_case to be called on line 27 within the friendly_id function. It works, but it's very wrong.

Here, we've abused use to inject functions such as title_case and dash_case into another module. It works, but we don't need to inject code at all. Elixir's import gives us all we need. Let's refactor the StringTransforms module to remove all code generation:

```elixir
defmodule StringTransforms do
  def title_case(str) do
    str
    |> String.split(" ")
    |> Enum.map(fn <<first::utf8, rest::binary>> ->
      String.upcase(List.to_string([first])) <> rest
    end)
    |> Enum.join(" ")
  end

  def dash_case(str) do
    str
    |> String.downcase
    |> String.replace(~r/[^\w]/, "-")
  end
  # ...
end

defmodule User do
  import StringTransforms

  def friendly_id(user) do
    dash_case(user.name)
  end
end

iex> User.friendly_id(%{name: "Elixir Lang"})
"elixir-lang"
```

We removed the __using__ block and relied on import to share our functions in the User module. Import gives us everything we had in our previous solution while allowing all string functions to be defined as regular definitions in the StringTransforms module. The use macro should never be used solely for mix-in style functionality. Importing functions serves the same purpose without generating code. Even for cases where you need use for code generation, you should only inject code that requires it, and you should import the rest as normal functions.

Avoid Injecting Large Amounts of Code

One common mistake that many people make with code generation is doing too much of it. Let's say you've weighed the pros and cons, and you know macros are required to solve your problem. The mistake you might make at this point is to go all out with quote blocks and inject hundreds of lines of code. This can make your code fragile and impossible to debug. Whenever you're injecting code, it should be your goal to delegate out of the caller's context as soon as possible. This way, your library code stays in your library, and the injected code is just the bare minimum to call out from the caller's context into your library functions.

To give you an idea of this design process, consider the email library that we envisioned in *To DSL or Not to DSL?*, on page 91. Even though it wouldn't make a good DSL, let's imagine how we would implement it as a macro-enhanced library. The library will need to inject a send_email function into a caller's module where functions can be defined to send different types of messages. The send_email function will apply email provider configuration for connecting to a mail service. Your first pass at this would probably use code generation all the way:

```
defmodule Emailer do
  defmacro __using__(config) do
    quote do
      def send_email(to, from, subject, body) do
        host = Dict.fetch!(unquote(config), :host)
        user = Dict.fetch!(unquote(config), :username)
        pass = Dict.fetch!(unquote(config), :password)

        :gen_smtp_client.send({to, [from], subject}, [
          relay: host,
          username: user,
          password: pass
        ])
      end
    end
  end
end
```

Your library could then be used by a client's MyMailer module:

```
defmodule MyMailer do
  use Emailer, username: "myusername",
               password: "mypassword",
               host: "smtp.example.com"

  def send_welcome_email(user) do
    send_email user.email, "support@example.com", "Welcome!", """
    Welcome aboard! Thanks for signing up...
    """
  end
end
```

At first glance, it might not look too bad. You're injecting send_email into the caller's module, and it's only a handful of lines of code. But don't fall into this trap. The issue is that the current implementation houses the validation of the configuration options as well as the details of sending an email directly in the injected code. This causes your implementation details to leak outside to every using module. It also makes your code harder to test.

Let's rewrite the library to delegate out of the caller's context to perform the email-sending work:

```
defmodule Emailer do
  defmacro __using__(config) do
    quote do
      def send_email(to, from, subject, body) do
        Emailer.send_email(unquote(config), to, from, subect, body)
      end
    end
  end

  def send_email(config, to, from, subject, body) do
    host = Dict.fetch!(config, :host)
    user = Dict.fetch!(config, :username)
    pass = Dict.fetch!(config, :password)

    :gen_smtp_client.send({to, [from], subject}, [
      relay: host,
      username: user,
      password: pass
    ])
  end
end
```

Notice how we pushed all the business logic and work of sending an email back into the Emailer module? The injected send_email/4 function delegates out immediately and passes along the caller's configuration. This subtle shift places all of the implementation concerns as a normal function definition on your library module. Your API remains exactly the same, but now you have the benefits of testing your Emailer.send_email/5 function directly. Another benefit is that stack traces now come from your Emailer module, not from a confusing generated code block within the caller's module.

This change also lets the library be called directly, without having to be used from another module. This is nice for testing, as well as for callers that only need to fire off quick emails. Sending email is now as simple as a call to your Emailer.send_email function:

```
[username: "myusername", password: "mypassword", host: "smtp.example.com"]
|> Emailer.send_email("you@example.com", "me@example.com", "Hi!", "")
```

If you use this delegation mindset when generating code, you'll end up with cleaner, testable, and debug-friendly libraries.

Kernel.SpecialForms: Know Your Environment and Limitations

Elixir is an incredibly extensible language, but even it has areas that are special and not overridable. Knowing where these are and why they exist will help keep you grounded in what is and isn't possible when extending the language. It will also help you keep track of where your code is executing.

The Kernel.SpecialForms module defines a set of constructs that you can't override. They make up the basic building blocks of the language and contain macros such as alias, case, {}, and <<>>. The SpecialForms module also includes a number of pseudo variables that contain information about the environment at compile time. You might already be familiar with a couple of these variables, such as __MODULE__ and __DIR__. The following pseudo variables are defined by SpecialForms and cannot be assigned to or overridden:

- __ENV__: Returns a Macro.ENV struct containing current environment information
- __MODULE__: Returns the current module name as an atom, equivalent to __ENV__.module
- __DIR__: Returns the current directory
- __CALLER__: Returns the caller's environment information as a Macro.ENV struct

The __ENV__ variable can be accessed at any time, but __CALLER__ can only be called within macros to return information about the caller's environment. These variables are used commonly with metaprogramming. The __before_compile__ hook that you first learned about in *Compile-Time Hooks*, on page 39, receives the __ENV__ struct as its only argument. This provides access to essential information about the environment that registered the hook.

Let's experiment with the __ENV__ struct in iex to see the kinds of information Elixir makes available to us:

```
iex(1)> __ENV__.file
"iex"

iex(2)> __ENV__.line
2

iex(3)> __ENV__.vars
[]

iex(4)> name = "Elixir"
"Elixir"

iex(5)> version = "~> 1.0"
"~> 1.0"

iex(6)> __ENV__.vars
[name: nil, version: nil]

iex(7)> binding
[name: "Elixir", version: "~> 1.0"]
```

You can see that even in iex, Elixir is tracking a file and a line number of the environment. In library code, this would be the actual file and line of the code you're working with. This can be useful for stack traces and special error handling, because you can have access to the caller's environment from elsewhere in your program. You can also see that Elixir tracks the bound variables of the current environment, which can be accessed from __ENV__.vars. Note that unlike the binding macro, which returns all bound variables with their values, the vars field tracks variable contexts instead. This is because a variable's value is dynamic at runtime, so the environment can track only which variables have been bound and from where.

There's little you can't override in Elixir—just a few special forms and the environment context. With such an extensible landscape, you've seen several ways it's easy to fall into trouble. But as a responsible metaprogrammer, you should also know that sometimes it's okay to push the limits.

Bending the Rules

That's the offical warning over with. So let's take a moment to remember that Elixir makes the world our playground. Rules are made to be broken. So here are some gray areas where abusing macros in Elixir is a worthy tradeoff, and some interesting ways we can bend Elixir's syntax.

Abusing Valid Elixir Syntax

Rewriting the AST to change the meaning of valid Elixir expressions probably sounds evil to most people. In some cases, it's actually a powerful tool. Consider Elixir's Ecto[2] library, which is a database wrapper and Language Integrated Query system. Let's take a look at what an Ecto query looks like to see how it abuses Elixir's syntax. You don't have to be familiar with Ecto; just be mindful of the query syntax in the following example:

```
query = from user in User,
    where: user.age > 21 and user.enrolled == true,
    select: user
```

Internally, Ecto converts this completely valid Elixir expression into a string of SQL. It abuses operators such as in, and, ==, and > to form SQL expressions out of valid Elixir code. This is an extremely neat use of macros. Ecto lets you build queries in Elixir's natural syntax, using bound variables that are typecasted appropriately in SQL. Other languages with a Language Integrated Query feature require an entirely new syntax on top of the language. With Elixir, we can use macros to change regular Elixir code into a SQL representation.

Ecto is a large project worthy of its own book, but let's imagine how we could implement a similar library. Let's see what the quoted form of our query above looks like. Try a few variations out in iex and think about ways you could use your AST tricks, such as Macro.postwalk from *Generate Less Code by Walking the AST*, on page 87.

```
iex> quote do
...>    from user in User,
...>       where: user.age > 21 and user.enrolled == true,
...>       select: user
...> end
{:from, [],
 [{:in, [context: Elixir, import: Kernel],
   [{:user, [], Elixir}, {:__aliases__, [alias: false], [:User]}]},
  [where: {:and, [context: Elixir, import: Kernel],
    [{:>, [context: Elixir, import: Kernel],
      [{{:., [], [{:user, [], Elixir}, :age]}, [], []}, 21]},
     {:==, [context: Elixir, import: Kernel],
      [{{:., [], [{:user, [], Elixir}, :enrolled]}, [], []}, true]}]},
   select: {:user, [], Elixir}]]}
```

Looking at the AST of an Ecto query, we can begin to see how macros would let us abuse Elixir syntax for fun and profit. By matching on the AST for dif-

---

2.   https://github.com/elixir-lang/ecto

ferent operators, such as :in, :==, and so on, we could parse the segments into the SQL representation at compile time. Macros allow any valid Elixir expression to be transformed into the requirements of your library. You must be careful with this technique, because giving language syntax new meaning in different contexts can become confusing. For libraries like Ecto, though, it's an extremely powerful way to build a new layer on top of Elixir without requiring any outside language additions.

Performance Optimization

Another area where you can bend the metaprogramming rules is performance optimizations. Macros let you optimize code at compile time, and sometimes this requires injecting larger amounts of code than usual. We bent this rule in our Translator library in *Building an Internationalization Library*, on page 49. Our implementation generated many function heads within the caller's module and also optimized string interpolation by replacing a regular expression at runtime with compile-time string concatenation. Fortunately, Elixir lends itself to fast execution without writing a bunch of dense code, but performance optimization comes at the cost of complexity. If you structure your metaprogramming using the tools you've learned, you should be able to produce fast code that's clear and maintainable.

Learn by Tinkering

Some of the greatest insights I've had with macros have been with irresponsible code that I would never ship to production. There's no substitute for learning by experimentation. Don't let the rules you've learned throughout this book and the hazards of this chapter scare you from fully exploring Elixir's macro system. Write irresponsible code, experiment, and have fun. Use the insight you gain to drive design decisions of things you would ship to a production system.

The possibilities for experimentation are endless, but here's a crazy idea to spike your imagination. Remember that any quoted expression is valid Elixir code? What if you exploited this fact to write a natural language test framework?

This is valid Elixir code:

```
the answer should be between 3 and 5
the list should contain 10
the user name should resemble "Max"
```

Don't believe me? Try quoting these expressions in iex:

```
iex> quote do
...>     the answer should be between 3 and 5
...>     the list should contain 10
...>     the user name should resemble "Max"
...> end |> Macro.to_string |> IO.puts
(
  the(answer(should(be(between(3 and 5)))))
  the(list(should(contain(10))))
  the(user(name(should(resemble("Max"))))))
)
:ok
```

You could parse the AST forms of these natural language declarations into assertions behind the scenes. Should you do this? Probably not. Would you gain new insight into Elixir's macro system and probably have some fun along the way? Absolutely.

Build the Future

What's next? It's time to head out there and build the future of Elixir software development! You now have the skills to shape the language and write powerful tools to share with the world. The programming landscape is ripe for disruption by the power that Elixir and the Erlang ecosystem bring to the table. Go out there and tackle interesting problems—and always remember to have fun.

Let's build the future!

Put the "Fun" in Functional

Elixir puts the "fun" back into functional programming, on top of the robust, battle-tested, industrial-strength environment of Erlang.

Programming Elixir

You want to explore functional programming, but are put off by the academic feel (tell me about monads just one more time). You know you need concurrent applications, but also know these are almost impossible to get right. Meet Elixir, a functional, concurrent language built on the rock-solid Erlang VM. Elixir's pragmatic syntax and built-in support for metaprogramming will make you productive and keep you interested for the long haul. This book is *the* introduction to Elixir for experienced programmers.

Maybe you need something that's closer to Ruby, but with a battle-proven environment that's unrivaled for massive scalability, concurrency, distribution, and fault tolerance. Maybe the time is right for the Next Big Thing. Maybe it's *Elixir*.

Dave Thomas
(340 pages) ISBN: 9781937785581. $36
https://pragprog.com/book/elixir

Programming Erlang (2nd edition)

A multi-user game, web site, cloud application, or networked database can have thousands of users all interacting at the same time. You need a powerful, industrial-strength tool to handle the really hard problems inherent in parallel, concurrent environments. You need Erlang. In this second edition of the best-selling *Programming Erlang*, you'll learn how to write parallel programs that scale effortlessly on multicore systems.

Joe Armstrong
(548 pages) ISBN: 9781937785536. $42
https://pragprog.com/book/jaerlang2

Seven in Seven

From Web Frameworks to Concurrency Models, see what the rest of the world is doing with this introduction to seven different approaches.

Seven Web Frameworks in Seven Weeks

Whether you need a new tool or just inspiration, *Seven Web Frameworks in Seven Weeks* explores modern options, giving you a taste of each with ideas that will help you create better apps. You'll see frameworks that leverage modern programming languages, employ unique architectures, live client-side instead of server-side, or embrace type systems. You'll see everything from familiar Ruby and JavaScript to the more exotic Erlang, Haskell, and Clojure.

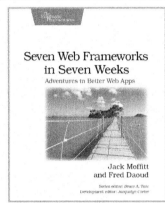

Jack Moffitt, Fred Daoud
(302 pages) ISBN: 9781937785635. $38
https://pragprog.com/book/7web

Seven Concurrency Models in Seven Weeks

Your software needs to leverage multiple cores, handle thousands of users and terabytes of data, and continue working in the face of both hardware and software failure. Concurrency and parallelism are the keys, and *Seven Concurrency Models in Seven Weeks* equips you for this new world. See how emerging technologies such as actors and functional programming address issues with traditional threads and locks development. Learn how to exploit the parallelism in your computer's GPU and leverage clusters of machines with MapReduce and Stream Processing. And do it all with the confidence that comes from using tools that help you write crystal clear, high-quality code.

Paul Butcher
(296 pages) ISBN: 9781937785659. $38
https://pragprog.com/book/pb7con

Past and Present

To see where we're going, remember how we got here, and learn how to take a healthier approach to programming.

Fire in the Valley

In the 1970s, while their contemporaries were protesting the computer as a tool of dehumanization and oppression, a motley collection of college dropouts, hippies, and electronics fanatics were engaged in something much more subversive. Obsessed with the idea of getting computer power into their own hands, they launched from their garages a hobbyist movement that grew into an industry, and ultimately a social and technological revolution. What they did was invent the personal computer: not just a new device, but a watershed in the relationship between man and machine. This is their story.

Michael Swaine and Paul Freiberger
(424 pages) ISBN: 9781937785765. $34
https://pragprog.com/book/fsfire

The Healthy Programmer

To keep doing what you love, you need to maintain your own systems, not just the ones you write code for. Regular exercise and proper nutrition help you learn, remember, concentrate, and be creative—skills critical to doing your job well. Learn how to change your work habits, master exercises that make working at a computer more comfortable, and develop a plan to keep fit, healthy, and sharp for years to come.

This book is intended only as an informative guide for those wishing to know more about health issues. In no way is this book intended to replace, countermand, or conflict with the advice given to you by your own healthcare provider including Physician, Nurse Practitioner, Physician Assistant, Registered Dietician, and other licensed professionals.

Joe Kutner
(254 pages) ISBN: 9781937785314. $36
https://pragprog.com/book/jkthp

Be Agile

Don't just "do" agile; you want to *be* agile. We'll show you how, for new code and old.

Your Code As a Crime Scene

Jack the Ripper and legacy codebases have more in common than you'd think. Inspired by forensic psychology methods, this book teaches you strategies to predict the future of your codebase, assess refactoring direction, and understand how your team influences the design. With its unique blend of forensic psychology and code analysis, this book arms you with the strategies you need, no matter what programming language you use.

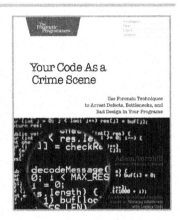

Adam Tornhill
(190 pages) ISBN: 9781680500387. $36
https://pragprog.com/book/atcrime

The Nature of Software Development

You need to get value from your software project. You need it "free, now, and perfect." We can't get you there, but we can help you get to "cheaper, sooner, and better." This book leads you from the desire for value down to the specific activities that help good Agile projects deliver better software sooner, and at a lower cost. Using simple sketches and a few words, the author invites you to follow his path of learning and understanding from a half century of software development and from his engagement with Agile methods from their very beginning.

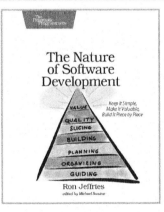

Ron Jeffries
(150 pages) ISBN: 9781941222379. $24
https://pragprog.com/book/rjnsd

Get Kids into Programming

Get your kids writing Minecraft plugins in Java, or 3D games in JavaScript. No experience required!

Learn to Program with Minecraft Plugins (2nd edition)

The bestselling, kid-tested book for Minecraft is now updated for CanaryMod! Write your own Minecraft plugins and watch your code come to life with flaming cows, flying creepers, teleportation, and interactivity. Add your own features to the Minecraft game by developing Java code that

Andy Hunt
(300 pages) ISBN: 9781941222942. $29
https://pragprog.com/book/ahmine2

3D Game Programming for Kids

You know what's even better than playing games? Creating your own. Even if you're an absolute beginner, this book will teach you how to make your own online games with interactive examples. You'll learn programming using nothing more than a browser, and see cool, 3D results as you type. You'll learn real-world programming skills in a real programming language: JavaScript, the language of the web. You'll be amazed at what you can do as you build interactive worlds and fun games. Appropriate for ages 10-99!

Printed in full color.

Chris Strom
(250 pages) ISBN: 9781937785444. $36
https://pragprog.com/book/csjava

The Pragmatic Bookshelf

The Pragmatic Bookshelf features books written by developers for developers. The titles continue the well-known Pragmatic Programmer style and continue to garner awards and rave reviews. As development gets more and more difficult, the Pragmatic Programmers will be there with more titles and products to help you stay on top of your game.

Visit Us Online

This Book's Home Page
https://pragprog.com/book/cmelixir
Source code from this book, errata, and other resources. Come give us feedback, too!

Register for Updates
https://pragprog.com/updates
Be notified when updates and new books become available.

Join the Community
https://pragprog.com/community
Read our weblogs, join our online discussions, participate in our mailing list, interact with our wiki, and benefit from the experience of other Pragmatic Programmers.

New and Noteworthy
https://pragprog.com/news
Check out the latest pragmatic developments, new titles and other offerings.

Save on the eBook

Save on the eBook versions of this title. Owning the paper version of this book entitles you to purchase the electronic versions at a terrific discount.

PDFs are great for carrying around on your laptop—they are hyperlinked, have color, and are fully searchable. Most titles are also available for the iPhone and iPod touch, Amazon Kindle, and other popular e-book readers.

Buy now at *https://pragprog.com/coupon*

Contact Us

Online Orders:	*https://pragprog.com/catalog*
Customer Service:	*support@pragprog.com*
International Rights:	*translations@pragprog.com*
Academic Use:	*academic@pragprog.com*
Write for Us:	*http://write-for-us.pragprog.com*
Or Call:	+1 800-699-7764

CPSIA information can be obtained at www.ICGtesting.com
Printed in the USA
BVOW09s0341221215

430723BV00013B/105/P

9 781680 500417